SCIENCE GIANTS
EARTH & SPACE

25 Activites Exploring the World's Greatest Scientific Discoveries

ALAN TICOTSKY

A GOOD YEAR BOOK™

Good Year Books
Tucson, Arizona

KH

Dedication

*To the giants upon whose shoulders I have stood,
in memory of Mary and Tye and Freema, and to Milton,
who continues to inspire and guide me.*

Good Year Books

Our titles are available for most basic curriculum subjects plus many enrichment areas. For more Good Year Books, contact your local bookseller or educational dealer. For a complete catalog with information about other Good Year Books, please contact:

Good Year Books
P.O. Box 91858
Tucson, AZ 85752-1858
www.goodyearbooks.com

Cover design: Sean O'Neill
Interior design: Dan Miedaner
Illustrations: Sean O'Neill
Cover Image Credits: Left to right, top: Engraving of Nicolaus Copernicus by French School, (16th Century), Bibliotheque Nationale, Paris, France/The Bridgeman Art Library; Photograph of Henrietta Leavitt courtesy of The American Association of Variable Star Observers (AAVSO); Engraving of Galileo Galilei by Robert Hart/Courtesy of Library of Congress
Left to right, bottom: Lithograph of Sir Francis Bacon, Viscount St. Albans, from 'Lodge's British Portraits', 1823 by Paul van Somer, ©Private Collection/Ken Welsh/The Bridgeman Art Library; Engraving of the Bust of Xenophanes by French School, (18th century), Bibliotheque Nationale, Paris, France/The Bridgeman Art Library

ISBN-10 1-59647-077-1
ISBN-13 978-1-59647-077-4

1 2 3 4 5 6 7 8 9 - ML - 09 08 07 06

8/22/06

Contents

Introduction for Teachers

Some ideas people believed in the past appear foolish to us. Other ideas seem to be inevitable but erroneous conclusions reached using limited resources and information. One may assume with reasonable certainty that some of today's prevailing knowledge will be overturned by new discoveries in the future. Science can describe reality to the limit of our tools and our ability to conceptualize that which we cannot measure or observe. New ideas constantly challenge old assumptions. Revolutions occur when an idea is discarded in favor of a better one.

The Structure of This Book

Science Giants: Earth and Space arranges important scientific discoveries in major disciplines into a historical context. Activities and simulations provide hands-on experiences for students using readily available classroom supplies. Activities are followed by student reading pages summarizing the history of scientific discovery and explaining the theories.

The book is divided into chapters based on major areas of science inquiry. Each chapter contains teacher instructions for active student investigations paired with student reading pages. You can use chapters individually, or you can follow the sequence of the book to provide an overview of the history of earth and space science.

Activities are designed for teams of students and follow a simple format—a list of materials needed per team (mostly common, inexpensive items), followed by instructions and teacher background information. Teamwork among students provides valuable rewards in the classroom. Working in teams:

- encourages dialogue among students, creating better thinking and more discovery.
- improves communication skills.
- increases motivation.
- promotes peer teaching and learning.
- builds social competency.

After doing an activity, hand out the student reading pages to enhance students' knowledge of the history behind each discovery. Student reading pages include vocabulary words, which are shown in bold type and defined at the end of each reading, and offer suggestions for further study. Time lines at the beginning of each chapter provide reference points and springboards for studying biography, an important and interesting aspect of the history of science. There's a bibliography for teachers at the end of the book.

The book focuses on ideas rather than personalities. Some famous legends are covered because scientific and historical literacy would be incomplete without them. The circumstances of discovery often illustrate the truth of Louis Pasteur's observation, ". . . chance favors the prepared mind." Using *Science Giants* should help prepare the minds of students for future discoveries.

Gender Equity

Why is there a predominance of men in the history of science? Margaret Cavendish appeared before the prestigious Royal Society in 1667; the first women were admitted as members in 1945. Examples of women scientists are necessary and important for students—and so is a discussion about why such a high percentage of great scientists mentioned in the history books are men.

As you and your students follow modern scientific developments in newspapers, magazines, and other media, note how both women and men contribute to the advances in all fields. Make it an assumption in your class: scientists come in all genders and colors and from all countries—in short, every variety of human being. Resources abound to help you if you choose to devote a section of study exclusively to women's contributions to science.

Generating Enthusiasm

Start each section with students' questions and ideas. What do they know? What do they want to know? Then go on and survey the history of each field you choose. The activities will emphasize science process skills and most will need little introduction—get the kids started and stay out of the way. Through the experimenting, students will be controlling variables, making predictions, recording and interpreting data, drawing conclusions, and *doing* science.

Connecting the main ideas in a historical and social context should enrich their overall understanding and make them eager to discover where science is heading today. Studying today's news should be a major goal for all of us who teach and especially those who teach science—helping students become scientifically literate and able to understand current issues and ideas.

As Isaac Newton once said, "If I have seen further, it is by standing on the shoulders of giants." A goal of writing and using this book is to excite the scientists of tomorrow about all there is to know now and all there is for them to discover in the future. There's a lot you can see from the shoulders of giants.

From *Science Giants: Earth and Space* © Good Year Books.

Introduction for Students

Science as Historical Process

What do we know and how do we know it? These two questions can lead you on a very rewarding journey. Thanks to thousands or even more years of questioning, observing, and experimenting, we know a mind-boggling amount about the world and universe around us. The average ten-year-old school child knows more science than anyone knew just a few hundred years ago. How did all that knowledge get here?

Isaac Newton (1642–1727) was born in the same year in which another famous scientist, Galileo Galilei (1564–1642), died. Responding to a question about how he could know so much, Newton is reported to have said, "If I have seen further, it is by standing on the shoulders of giants." Galileo was a giant pair of shoulders for Newton, and Newton grew giant shoulders for others. Every generation starts from the current knowledge and builds further.

Look outside your classroom window. The sun comes up on one side of the building, rises and travels across the sky, then heads down to set on another side. Throughout the year, the sun's path changes as it appears lower in the winter and higher in the summer. Doesn't it seem reasonable to describe the sun as traveling around the Earth?

In fact, not so long ago, most people thought the Earth was the center of the universe. Other ideas that have changed include the following:

- Scientists believe the Earth was formed about five billion years ago. In 1650, Bishop Ussher set the date at 4004 B.C.
- Things burn when they combine with *oxygen*, not because they contain a substance called *phlogiston*.
- Matter consists of tiny atoms that are themselves made of smaller substances. Earlier people believed all matter was made from four elements: earth, fire, water, and air.
- Plants make their own food mostly out of the carbon in the air, not from the soil or water.

Who knows what ideas of today will be changed in the future? Enjoy these activities and ideas that teach about how science has grown and changed, and maybe you will see something new on the shoulders of giants.

The Universe

TIME LINE

Year	Notable Event
8000 B.C.	Central American civilizations built structures aligned with celestial objects.
4000 B.C.	Egyptians devised a calendar based on the sun and stars. Over time, they built pyramids aligned with sky objects.
2800 B.C.	Stonehenge was built in England.
2296 B.C.	Chinese observers tracked a comet.
A.D. 150	Claudius Ptolemy wrote an astronomy book that was accepted as a text for hundreds of years. The Earth was considered to be the center of the universe.
1543	Nicolaus Copernicus published his theory that the Earth and other planets orbit the sun.
1577	Tycho Brahe determined that a comet was farther from Earth than the moon.
1609	Galileo Galilei built a telescope and the next year published *The Starry Messenger,* which described his discoveries with his telescope.
1618	Johannes Kepler published his theories, one of which stated that planets travel in elliptical orbits.
1656	Christiaan Huygens observed the rings of Saturn.
1682	Edmond Halley observed a comet and predicted its return.
1687	Isaac Newton published the *Principia* containing theories of gravity and orbital motion.
1781	William Herschel observed Uranus.
1846	Johan Galle observed Neptune using calculations from Urbain Leverrier and John Couch Adams.
1912	Henrietta Leavitt studied Cepheid variable stars and devised a way to measure their distance from Earth.
1927	Georges Lemaitre theorized that the universe began with a large explosion, now popularly called the "Big Bang."
1929	Edwin Hubble confirmed that the universe is expanding.
1930	Clyde Tombaugh discovered Pluto.
1969	Neil Armstrong and Buzz Aldrin landed on the moon.

Materials per Team

- round balloons
- soft-tipped markers

The Big Bang

An Expanding Universe

This activity has two parts. The first illustrates the movement of matter away from the site of the so-called Big Bang, a primeval occurrence scientists theorize may have formed the universe. The second simulates how wavelength changes as objects move in relation to each other.

Activity 1

To illustrate the concept of an expanding universe, use balloons to simulate movement in all directions from a central beginning point. Have students make small dots on the surface of uninflated balloons. As they blow air into the balloons, ask them to observe how the dots move away from each other and from the center of the balloon. The dots may represent stars or galaxies of stars.

Activity 2

When objects move away from us, the waves we receive from them seem to lengthen. That is, the distance between the peaks of the waves spreads out because their source is receding. This is similar to the Doppler effect in sound waves. The pitch of a train whistle or emergency vehicle siren seems to change as it moves either toward or away from the listener.

Students can simulate this lengthening or shortening of waves. Designate one person as a receiver on Earth. Group another few students several steps away to represent the waves from a star. Ask one person from the star to walk toward the receiver at a constant rate while the rest of the group takes a step back in the other direction. Each time the star group recedes a step, another wave heads toward Earth, walking at the constant rate.

After repeating this process several times, students will note how much longer the waves are taking to reach the receiver and how the distance between the waves has increased. If the waves were light waves, the receiver would see a color shift. If they were sound waves, the pitch would change. Edwin Hubble used this method to theorize that the universe is expanding.

R E A D I N G:
The Origins of the Universe

How did the universe begin? Imagine designing a laboratory or classroom experiment to answer that! **Cosmology** is the name of the branch of science or philosophy that seeks to explain the origins of the universe. For as long as humans have recorded history, people have tried to follow time back to its beginnings. In modern scientific societies, the search continues.

Strangely, or perhaps not so strangely, the study of the very smallest components of matter lead scientists to discoveries about the very vastness of the universe. The huge amount of energy that can be released from tiny atoms suggests theories about a possible "Big Bang" origin of the universe. Perhaps an explosion occurred when all matter was once densely packed in an incredibly small area.

Every culture seems to have a version of how the Earth and sky were created. You have probably read creation stories from cultures around the world. Ask your librarian or teacher to help you find a few and compare the various stories.

The ancient Greeks, Arabs, and Chinese, especially, studied the skies intensely. The Egyptian pyramids and prehistoric stone monuments such as Stonehenge in England line up with **astronomical** positions. Scientists continue to study these impressive ancient achievements to learn how much people knew about the universe. Eratosthenes (276–195 B.C.) estimated the size of the Earth fairly accurately by comparing shadow lengths in two places on the same day. He reasoned that the difference in shadows indicated that the Earth was not flat, but spherical.

Much of the knowledge of the ancients was lost or ignored for centuries. Superstition and **dogma** (a set of ideas to be believed) dominated people's view of the universe. European science began to come alive again in the fifteenth and sixteenth centuries. During this time, which became known as the **Renaissance**, the stubbornly held idea of the Earth as the center of the universe began to be challenged.

Edmond Halley (1656–1742) explained comets and their long journeys. Comets orbit the sun but travel far beyond the outer planets on their journeys. Not only was the Earth's position as the center of the universe challenged, but its size was becoming ever more like that of a tiny seed afloat in a vast ocean.

In 1912 American Henrietta Leavitt (1868–1921) devised a method of measuring the distance of certain stars from Earth. These **Cepheid variable stars** change brightness over a period of time. Leavitt determined that the **Magellanic Clouds** are far beyond our galaxy. In 1929, fellow American Edwin Hubble (1889–1953) built upon her discoveries and proposed that the universe is not only bigger than Leavitt proved but that it is expanding.

Hubble reasoned that the **wavelength** of light received on Earth indicated that stars and galaxies were moving rapidly away from our planet. Since the nineteenth century, starlight could be broken into a **spectrum**, or rainbow. The spectrum's pattern can be analyzed to determine the chemical elements that make up the star. Hubble used the stars' light to determine that they are racing away from Earth.

Hubble's findings corroborated a 1927 theory of Belgian Georges Lemaître (1894–1966). Lemaître proposed that the universe was born in a great explosion, or Big Bang. By the later part of the twentieth century, most cosmologists had accepted the Big Bang theory. All the mass of the universe was packed into a tiny space and an unimaginably powerful explosion sent matter on its way. The universe is calculated to be more than ten billion years old, so the galaxies have been speeding away from each other for a long time.

Albert Einstein (1879–1955) connected mass and energy with his famous equation, $E = mc^2$, which means: Energy equals mass times the speed of light squared, or the speed of light multiplied by itself. Einstein proposed several remarkable theories and many important concepts came from them. For example, he claimed that gravity could affect light, and he was proven to be correct. His view of the universe was of a vast and expanding space with time as a fourth dimension.

What will be added to this modern creation story as more discoveries occur in the years to come?

Albert Einstein

Vocabulary Words

astronomical .... having to do with objects outside the Earth

Cepheid variable star .... giant stars that display a cycle of varying brightness

cosmology .... that branch of science the deals with the creation and evolution of the universe

dogma....................................... a set of ideas to be believed

Magellanic Clouds .... galaxies that are visible from the Southern Hemisphere

renaissance .... a revival; a reawakening of cultural achievement

spectrum .... sequence or range of energy by wavelength

wavelength .... distance between identical parts of waves, such as the distance between crests or between troughs

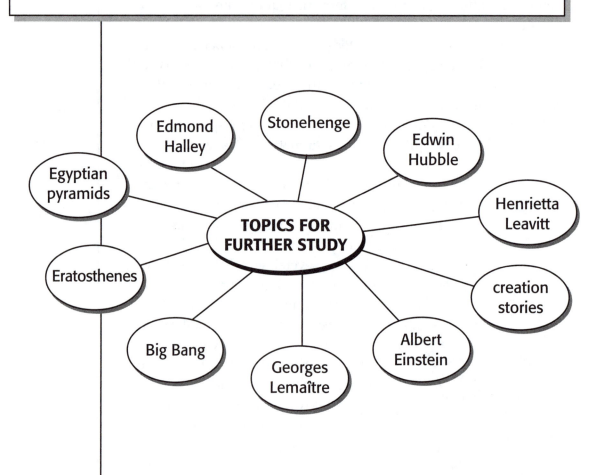

Earth and Shadows

The Reasons for Seasons

Materials per Team

- round balloons
- newspaper
- liquid starch
- tempera paint (optional)
- flashlights
- globe to use as a model
- large sheets of black paper
- chalk

Here are some suggestions to help students understand the reasons for seasons. The first set of activities uses a model of the Earth, and the second is a year-long shadow tracking project.

Activity 1

To appreciate the Earth's spherical shape, students can make models of our planet. The models will be useful manipulatives when studying the Earth and the solar system and will help them visualize our place in space.

Have students inflate a round balloon and tie it closed. They can then soak some newspaper strips in liquid starch and smooth them onto the balloon. After it hardens, they can paint their papier-mâché spheres to represent bodies of water, land, and ice.

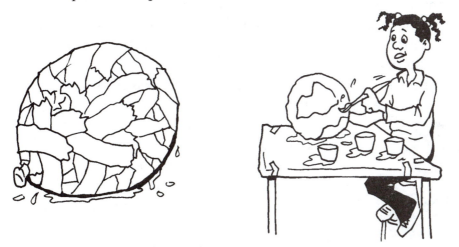

Use the Earth models and flashlights to demonstrate seasons and day and night. Have each team set a flashlight on a table and let it shine onto a model Earth. The flashlight beam hits directly on one part and other areas receive a less intense, more spread out light. When the sphere is tilted to about a 23° angle, students will see that seasons depend upon which pole is tilted toward the sun.

People in the Northern Hemisphere have summer when the North Pole is tipped toward the sun and winter when it is tipped away. For people in the Southern Hemisphere, the seasons are opposite because the South Pole tips in the opposite direction. Spring and fall occur when the Earth's axis points neither toward nor away from the sun and the strongest light beams strike the Earth near the equator.

Have one student from each team carry a model Earth around the flashlight "sun" while holding the angle of the Earth constant. Assign another team member to turn the flashlight so it shines on the Earth as it travels. Students will see that the tilt of the Earth on its axis causes different parts of the Earth to receive more or less sunlight during different seasons. Holding a toothpick or a play figure on the part of the world in which they live may help younger students understand the "reason for the seasons."

Activity 2

Another way to track the cyclical relationship of the seasons to the angle of the Earth's tilt is to measure shadows. Here's a suggestion that creates an effective display as the year goes along:

Choose one student and name the activity after him or her—for example, "Brian's Shadow." Once a month at noon (1 o'clock Daylight Time), go outside and have that student face south. Try to do this around the twenty-first of the month to be near solstices and equinoxes when they occur.

Trace the outline of the student's shadow with chalk on black paper. Cut out the shadow shape and hang it on a wall inside. How tall is the student, and how tall is the shadow? What happens each month? If you keep a graph of the number of hours of sunlight each day, the students will quickly see a correlation between that chart and the shadows throughout the year. The shadows themselves make an effective graph of the sun's behavior over time.

READING:
Why There Are Seasons

You knew more about the universe when you began first grade than most ancient people knew their whole lives. You notice the sun rise in the east, climb throughout the day, and set in the west. Our ancient ancestors saw this too, but you know something they probably didn't know; the sun doesn't travel around the Earth.

The Earth turns like a spinning ball and carries us along. It is as if we are riding on a merry-go-round. While the Earth turns toward the east, the sun (and, when we can see them at night, the other stars) appears to travel west. This is similar to the way trees seem to speed by when you look out the window of a car or train, but it is you who are moving, not the trees. Many ancient people never knew that the Earth travels around the sun.

Careful observation revealed predictable patterns of motion of the sun, moon, and stars. Day and night alternate. The sun appears to rise from the east each day and travel steadily across the sky, setting below the **horizon** in the west. As seasons progress, the sun appears to change its position slightly every day, moving north to south or vice versa. These regular and predictable movements helped establish **calendars** and planting schedules.

The moon not only changes its position, but its shape as well! Beginning as a small sliver or crescent, the moon grows into a full sphere. Then it gradually transforms to a mirror image of its young self before disappearing altogether. Meanwhile, the stars march across the night sky regularly, except for a few "wanderers" (planets) that behave differently.

In modern times, we know the explanations for these movements. The Earth spins, rotating once per day so that we see the sun go by as we ride on our turning sphere. Sometimes our view is toward the sun while at night we look out away from it. Imagine a ride on a merry-go-round. The fairgrounds seem to be moving past as the carousel turns. During one part of the ride, you might see the ferris wheel and during another part you see the midway.

In addition to spinning once every 24 hours, the Earth travels around, or orbits, the sun once every 365 1/4 days. The sun shines higher in the summer sky and drops closer to the horizon in the winter. Why? It is because the Earth is tilted on its North Pole–

South Pole axis, the imaginary line drawn through the planet. When our closer pole is tipped toward the sun, rays of light shine down more directly. When our pole tips away, we have to look toward the **equator** to see the source of our light.

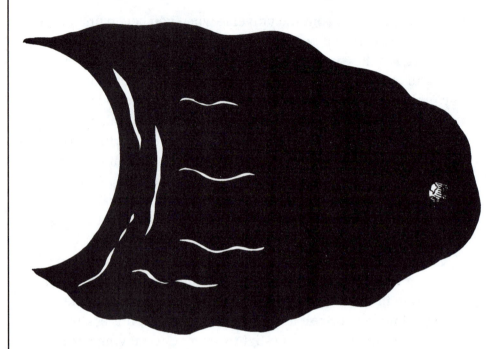

The apparent backward movements of some of the planets were hard to explain in ancient times. Believing that the sun is the center of a solar system allowed people to figure out what happens. While the Earth is turning once per day, it and all the other planets are orbiting the sun much like runners circle a track. The Earth takes an inside track on some of its neighbors (Mars, Jupiter, and Saturn were known since ancient times) and needs less time to complete one orbit. Our planet travels to the outside of Mercury and Venus, and those planets orbit the sun more quickly than we do.

Imagine the thinking it took to figure this out. The Greek astronomer Claudius Ptolemy (c. 100–170) described the universe as Earth-centered, and his view was accepted by many long into the Middle Ages. Nicolaus Copernicus (1473–1543) and Galileo Galilei (1564–1642) helped convince people that the Earth and other planets actually travel around the sun. If you read more about how they figured that out, and how angry the discovery made some people, you will appreciate how much courage it takes to change people's minds.

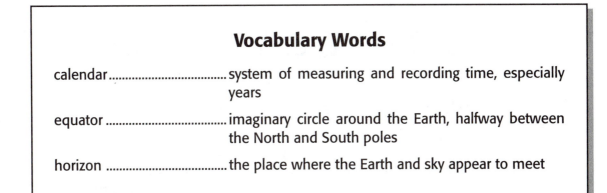

Vocabulary Words

calendar......................................system of measuring and recording time, especially years

equator ....imaginary circle around the Earth, halfway between the North and South poles

horizon ....the place where the Earth and sky appear to meet

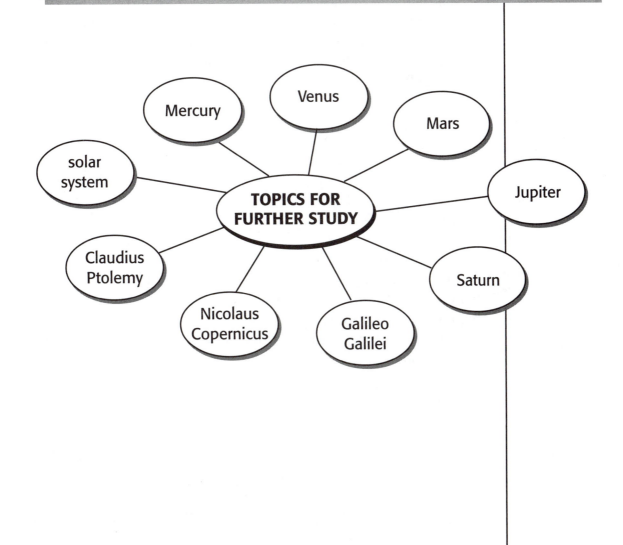

From *Science Giants: Earth and Space* © Good Year Books. This page may be reproduced for classroom use only by the actual purchaser of the book. www.goodyearbooks.com

Materials per Team

- soft wood or thick cardboard
- push pins
- string
- pencils and paper
- drawing compasses

Making an Ellipse

Not Quite a Circle

Planets do not orbit the sun in a circle but rather travel in an ellipse. Every point on a circle is the same distance from one specific point, the center. An ellipse has two key interior points called the *focuses,* or *foci.* From any point on an ellipse, the sum of the distances from that point to each of the foci is the same as from any other point. In this activity, students will try their hands at drawing ellipses.

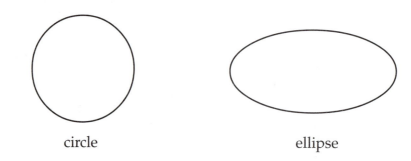

circle   ellipse

Have students practice drawing circles with compasses or by tying a string to a push pin and a pencil. Have them stick the push pin into paper or soft wood to establish the center of the circle. Tell them to keep the string stretched taut to its full length as they draw a circle around the pin.

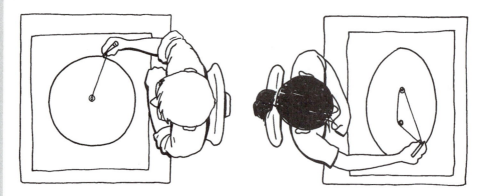

Then have them use two pins as focuses to draw an ellipse. Show how to tie string into a loop and lay it down around the pins. Have them stretch the string with a pencil, making sure it catches on both pins. When the string is taut, tell them to lower their pencil points and draw their ellipses.

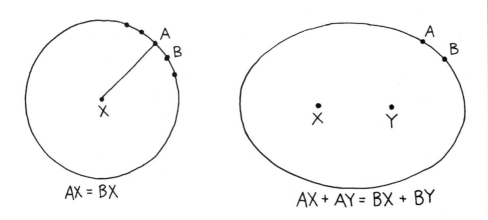

AX = BX   AX + AY = BX + BY

Earth's path brings it to within 147.1 million kilometers of the sun and as far away as 152.1 million kilometers. This is nearly circular, especially compared to Mercury, which comes as close as 45.9 million kilometers and moves as far as 69.7 million kilometers away from the sun.

R E A D I N G:
How the Planets Move

How do we know so much about how planets and other space objects move? After all, objects in the sky appear to circle the Earth. People figured out lots of interesting facts about planetary motion well before the invention of **satellites** and space travel.

In Europe during the **Middle Ages,** people were taught that the Earth was the center of the universe. That idea had been popularized by the Greek astronomer Claudius Ptolemy (c. 100–170). Nicolaus Copernicus (1473–1543), a Polish astronomer, figured out that the moon **orbited** the Earth, so he reasoned that the Earth and other planets might be orbiting the sun. Although this idea contradicted what most people in Europe had believed for well over a thousand years, it fit the data.

Copernicus was then able to account for the movement of other objects and published his theory in his important book, *On the Revolutions of the Heavenly Spheres.* But many of the authorities of Copernicus's time were opposed to his theories, and he did not publish the book until the year he died.

Tycho Brahe (1546–1601) observed the sky carefully and noted changes that occurred. His recording of a **supernova** helped make astronomy a science based on observation and data. Brahe's extensive collection of data helped make the case for a Copernican model rather than a Ptolemic one.

Galileo Galilei (1564–1642) further proved the accuracy of Copernicus's model. Galileo built **telescopes,** observed the sun, moon, Venus, and Jupiter closely, and gazed at the rings of Saturn.

But he too was attacked for his work. He was put on trial and died as a prisoner. He was forced to say the Earth was the center of the universe, but legend says he murmured, ". . . it does indeed move." In any case, Galileo's ideas survived and the power of truth could not be suppressed forever.

Galileo Galilei (engraving by Robert Hart, courtesy of Library of Congress)

Johannes Kepler (1571–1630) used math to help understand more about how the planets moved. He discovered that their orbits are not circles but ellipses. Years later, Kepler's important laws of planetary motion helped scientists discover the outer planets, send rockets to explore the solar system, and understand more clearly the paths the planets followed.

From the seventeenth century on, the pace of exploration sped up. So many new ideas were discovered that scientists felt freer to express their views and seek the facts. Isaac Newton (1642–1727) described gravity as the force that holds the solar system in place. Newton, born just after Galileo died, theorized that objects attract one another through the force of gravity. Gravity also controls the movement of planets and other orbiting bodies. Simply put, the Earth's gravity pulls the moon toward it, but the moon's orbiting motion prevents it from falling closer.

You could have gotten into a lot of trouble in the 1500s and 1600s for claiming that the Earth orbits the sun and that the sun is the center of our planetary system. Probably some of the ideas you think are true will be found to be wrong in the future. We should remember that we need to keep an open mind about ideas. In science, things change when a new theory comes along and explains things more clearly than an existing theory. When that happens, it could be time to change our thinking.

Vocabulary Words

Middle Ages .... historical period in Europe, from approximately A.D. 500–1500

orbited .... traveled around

satellite .... a man-made or natural object orbiting another object

supernova .... a star that suddenly becomes much brighter for a short time and then fades

telescope .... an instrument for viewing distant objects

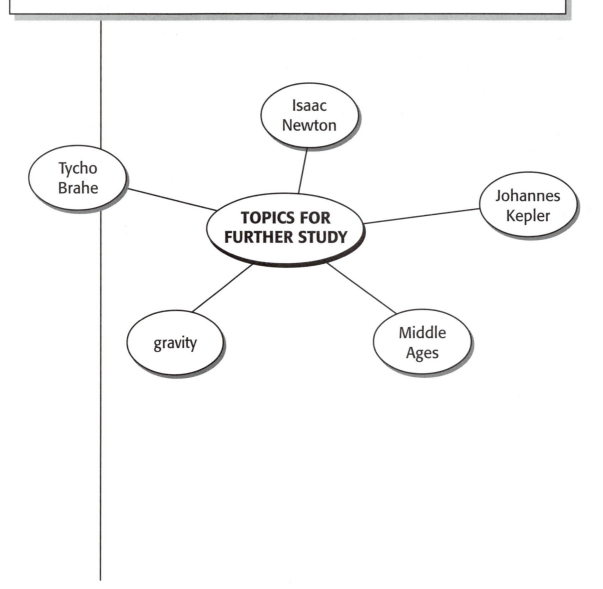

Moon Motion and Craters

Learning about Moons

The moon is our closest space neighbor. It has fascinated people for centuries. Find out what your students know about the moon and why they think it behaves the way it does. Careful observation and recording over the course of a month will teach students a lot about Earth's orbiting buddy. Mornings when the moon is visible are especially useful for school-time observing.

The moons of Jupiter helped Galileo Galilei clarify his thinking about the motions of bodies in the solar system. Here are three activities about moons. Two of them simulate the motion and the topography of the Earth's moon, and the other demonstrates how Galileo used his discovery of Jupiter's moons to deduce that the Earth is not the center of the universe.

Materials per Team

- flashlights (optional)
- aluminum pie tins
- flour or sand and a colored powder for contrast (colored sand, cinnamon, ground pepper . . .)
- newspaper

Activity 1

Divide the class into groups of three. One student will be the sun, another the Earth, and the third will be the moon (see the illustration on page 22). Because the number of revolutions is so high, players will only act out part of a lunar and planetary cycle.

The moon will slowly circle the Earth in a counterclockwise direction, always facing the same side of the Earth. (Here, all directions are referenced as if you are looking down upon the Earth and moon from above their north poles.) The Earth, meanwhile, is doing its own traveling: It orbits the sun in a counter-clockwise direction and spins counterclockwise while orbiting.

Here are the relative times each celestial object requires to complete a cycle of its movements: The Earth will spin 28 times while the moon orbits it once. The moon will orbit the Earth about 13 times while the Earth completes one trip around the sun. The Earth will spin 365 times during its revolution around the sun.

The person representing the sun can aim a flashlight at the Earth and moon to demonstrate how people on Earth only see a portion of the moon most of the time. Have students switch places to take on each role.

As an extension, tell students that the sun does its own celestial touring, as a part of the spiraling Milky Way galaxy that rotates and travels toward other parts of space. The sun is so massive that its gravity pulls the whole solar system along with it on its journey.

Activity 2

The moon has a stark landscape pockmarked with rugged craters. Students can simulate the formation of craters using common materials.

Have students spread some flour or sand in an aluminum pie tin. They can place the pie tin on some newspaper to catch any wayward powder. When they drop a marble or small stone onto the surface of the flour, a crater forms. Have them practice changing the angle of landing and the size of the "meteorite."

To increase contrast and see how far the impact propels surface dust, have students spread a layer of a different-colored powder on top of an area of the flour. The resulting crater will stand out from the rest of the landscape.

Activity 3

Although he was most likely not the first person to build a telescope, Galileo used his invention to study the objects in space and made several important discoveries. He studied Earth's moon extensively and changed its image from a magical being to a hunk of orbiting rock. The crater activity will give students an idea of what he saw through his telescope.

Galileo is credited with discovering the moons of Jupiter, spotting at least four of them. Students can once again simulate moon motion to learn what Galileo learned, but this time the moons will be orbiting Jupiter.

Divide the players into teams of five. Place large dividers (such as mobile chalkboards) in places where students can walk around them on all sides. These large objects will represent Jupiter. Have the teams make signs to carry to represent the four largest moons of Jupiter, which were the ones Galileo could see through his telescope. Their names are Ganymede, Io, Europa, and Callisto.

Teams can look up the statistics of Jupiter's moons before playing, or you may choose to use the chart on page 25. Each line in the chart represents one day in a typical month. Assume that the person who made the chart observed the moons at the same time each night. The chart shows the positions of the moons appear as they would to an observer using a telescope. Because telescopes reverse the view, the moons appear to orbit in a counterclockwise direction.

Have students who are playing the role of moons walk counterclockwise around the large object in your classroom representing Jupiter and stand left to right in the order indicated by the order of letters in the chart. When the name of one of the moons is in brackets [ ], the moon is hidden behind the moon next to it or behind Jupiter. Moons in front of Jupiter are indicated in bold; an observer with a powerful enough telescope would see them as spots on the planet.

Assign one player on each team the role of Galileo on Earth. Galileo watches as the others carry the moon signs around Jupiter. After recording the positions for several revolutions, Galileo can share the data with the team and work collaboratively to write a persuasive letter explaining why the Earth is not the center of the universe.

The political and church leaders of Galileo's time made him retract his statements because they were so revolutionary and disturbing. Discuss with students how new scientific discoveries can be threatening to current government leaders.

Jupiter

The Moons of Jupiter

Day of the Month		Jupiter Position	
1	C	**J**	I E G
2	C E	[I]	G
3	E I	[C]	G
4	G	**J**	I E C
5	G I	**E**	C
6	G E	**J**	I C
7	I	[G]	E C
8		**J**	I E G C
9	E I	**J**	G C
10	E	**J**	I G C
11	G	[I]**C**	E
12	G C I	**J**	E
13	C G E	**J**	I
14	C I G	**J**	E
15	C	**J**	I G [E]
16	C E [I]	**J**	G
17	C E	**J**	I G
18	C [I]G	**J**	E
19	G C	**I**	E
20	G E	**J**	I C
21	G I	[E]	C
22		**J**	I G E C
23	I E	**J**	G C
24	E	**J**	I G C
25	I	**J**	G E C
26	G	**I**	E C
27	G E	**J**	I C
28	G [E] I	**C**	
29	C	**J**	G I E
30	C I E	**J**	G
31	C E	**J**	I G

C = Callisto   I = Io   E = Europa   G = Ganymede

[ ] means moon is hidden behind Jupiter or another moon

BOLD means moon is in front of Jupiter or another moon

READING:
Our Neighbor, the Moon

Take a good look at the moon. Note what time of day or night it is where you are. What shape is the lighted part of the moon? Try to look for the moon at the same time for a few days and observe how its position and shape keep changing.

What does the surface look like? Until the early 1600s, people used only their eyes to see the moon. When **refracting telescopes** were made and used by inventors like Hans Lippershey (c. 1570–1619) and Galileo Galilei (1564–1642), surface features seemed to jump out. The telescope's lenses bent light rays, enlarging the images they carried. The lunar terrain appeared stark and barren, but not totally unlike some of the harsher regions of Earth. The moon seemed less magical but perhaps even more mysterious.

Isaac Newton (1642–1727) devised a **reflecting** telescope, which further improved the view from Earth. Newton's design involved mirrors that focused the distant images and magnified them. Greater surface detail than ever was available to the human eye.

A legendary story in science tells us that Newton watched a falling apple and compared its motion to the moon's. Gravity pulls both the apple and the moon toward Earth. But while the apple hits the Earth (or Newton), the moon does not. Newton reasoned that **orbital motion** keeps the moon in space while it continues to fall around the Earth. His great leap of understanding led to a new theory of planetary motion controlled by gravity.

Why does the moon appear so battered and rugged compared to the Earth? For many years it was a dream that someone would travel to the moon and check out the landscape. Some fanciful theories suggested that large bodies of water (each one named a *mare,* or sea) existed there.

When a piece of space rock heads for Earth, it must travel through the **atmosphere.** Friction is created between the gasses in the atmosphere and the **meteorite.** This usually causes the rock to burn into tiny harmless particles. At night, these meteorites leave beautiful flaming trails we call shooting stars. If you stargaze regularly, you are bound to see them occasionally.

The moon lacks the truly protective atmosphere we have here on Earth. A meteorite headed toward the moon will not burn up and may well score a forceful direct hit, resulting in an **impact crater.** Galileo studied the craters and mountains of the moon through his telescope and published paintings of what he saw.

When Galileo discovered the moons of Jupiter, he helped disprove the theory that Earth was the center of the universe. Worse yet, people could no longer claim that Earth had the only moon. Galileo's telescope revealed four moons that orbited Jupiter and moved across the sky with it. Jupiter's four largest moons are named Ganymede, Io, Europa, and Callisto. The largest craters on our moon are easily seen from Earth and can be studied with a pair of **binoculars.** Compare the view using just your eyes at first. Choose a spot on the moon to observe, and then hold up the binoculars and see the details appear.

The power of increase should be marked on the binoculars—for example, 7X means "seven power." In that case, the object viewed appears seven times larger, or closer, than it did to your unaided eyes. Assuming the moon is about 240,000 miles (about 375,000 kilometers) away, divide that number by the viewing power to calculate how close to the moon your binoculars seem to take you.

In the 1950s, the Soviet Union and the United States began to send satellites into orbit and soon people were riding in the space crafts. In the early 1960s, President John F. Kennedy (1917–1963) challenged his nation to send an astronaut to the moon before the next decade. On July 20, 1969, the challenge was met when Neil Armstrong (b. 1930) and Edwin "Buzz" Aldrin (b. 1930) explored the surface of the moon while Michael Collins (b. 1930) orbited above the surface in the return vehicle. Scientists actually received moon rocks to study when the space travelers returned.

In the early twentieth century, unmanned space crafts began once again to visit and explore Mars. People will always dream of exploring new parts of the universe. As technology improves, so do the chances of humans leaving the Earth for other regions. Science fiction has a way of turning into reality after a while.

Vocabulary Words

atmosphere .... envelope of gasses surrounding a body in space

binoculars .... optical device used for magnifying objects at distances. Binoculars consist of two telescope-like tubes, one for each eye.

impact crater .... geologic feature caused by a large object from space crashing into the surface of a planet or moon

mare .... Latin for "sea," a term used to describe and name the flat plains on the moon

meteorite .... object from space that has reached Earth

orbital motion .... the path of an object as it revolves around another object

reflecting .... bouncing off; throwing back

refracting .... bending of light as it passes from one medium to another

telescope .... an instrument for detecting and viewing distant objects

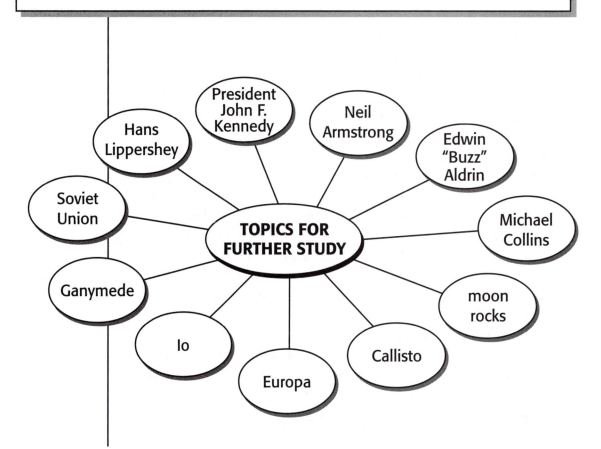

Discovering a Planet

How to Tell a Star from a Planet

Materials per Team

- star charts
- a photocopier

When objects in the sky are too small to be viewed in detail, how do observers determine whether they are stars or nearby neighbors such as planets or asteroids? In this activity, students will make drawings of the night sky to simulate a method astronomers use to differentiate "local" objects from the background field of stars.

Provide or have students find charts of the night sky. These are available from the newspaper, astronomy magazines, encyclopedias, the Internet, or stargazing books from the library. Have each group draw the stars without connecting them into constellations, or provide photocopies and ask students to add some stars of their own onto the charts. To vary the activity, use different charts—for example, use star maps from different seasons, or showing different parts of the sky (north, south, east, and west). The brightest stars can be represented as larger dots, and students should add a few background stars not usually considered part of the constellations. Make the charts more complicated for older students and use fewer stars for younger students.

After every group has completed its own star chart, photocopy each chart twice and return them to the groups. Pretend these are photographs of the night sky. On one copy, each group should draw a new "star." This new dot will represent a planet. Because

our eyes do not distinguish the difference between planets and stars, students don't have to draw their planets any differently from the other stars. Groups should label their charts "1." On the second photocopy, have each group draw their planet in a different spot. The change in position represents the planet's motion from the time the first "photograph" was taken until the second image was taken. Label these charts "2."

Photocopy both new versions of the star charts after the students have added planets so that the color of the drawn object does not stand out. Keep the pairs of charts together. Switch papers among groups and let students try to find the added planets other teams have drawn.

Careful observation can reveal which star is a "wanderer" and therefore not really a star but a planet. This simulates the method used by Clyde Tombaugh when he discovered Pluto in 1930. Comparing photographic plates of the heavens, Tombaugh saw the motion of the planet against the background of stars.

Pluto

READING:
Knowing Our Place in Space

The name *planet* comes from a Greek word meaning "wanderer." When viewed by people on Earth, planets appear to move differently than stars do. Sometimes they move backward, or east across the sky, but then they reverse motion and head west. Mercury and Venus, for example, sometimes appear as morning stars and sometimes as evening stars, but they never spend the whole night shining for us to see.

Nicolaus Copernicus (1473–1543) studied the motion of the planets. Copernicus figured out that the moon **orbited** the Earth, so he tried imagining the Earth and other planets orbiting the sun. This scheme explained the motion of the planets much more completely than the model that placed the Earth in the center. Because this change of thinking upset many people, Copernicus withheld publication of his ideas until his death. But the truth was too hard to suppress.

The telescope helped astronomers discover the planets beyond Saturn, as did the laws of gravity. William Herschel (1738–1822) discovered Uranus in 1781 by noting its motion. Later, Neptune's existence was confirmed after Alexis Bouvard (1767–1843) predicted it would be there—some massive object was affecting the orbit of Uranus. It turned out to be another planet.

Astronomers continued looking outward. An astronomer named Clyde Tombaugh (1906–1997) discovered Pluto in 1930 by carefully analyzing photographs of the night sky. He saw that one of the "stars" in the photo was a wanderer, moving differently from the others.

Stars also appear to change position because of the Earth's movements. In the course of one night, stars seem to travel from east to west across the sky because we on Earth are turning beneath them. The Earth's rotation carries us toward the east. From night to night, stars appear to shift farther west. Again, our spaceship Earth causes this by carrying us counterclockwise around the sun when viewed from above the North Pole. Each

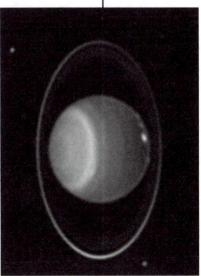

Uranus
(courtesy of NASA)

night when we look up to the stars, they seem to have shifted because we have traveled through space and are viewing them from a slightly different perspective.

Planets orbit the sun and are much closer to us on Earth than any star except the sun. Mercury and Venus are closer to the sun than Earth and therefore take a shorter time to complete one orbit than our planet. It is as if they are racing on shorter inside tracks. Sometimes we see them in the morning and sometimes in the evening, but never in the darkest hours of night when we are looking out away from the sun.

During those nighttime hours, we may see the planets Mars, Jupiter, or Saturn, which all have longer orbits than Earth. Of the three outermost planets, only Uranus is a bright enough target for our unaided eyes to see. Sometimes we are overtaking one of those solar system neighbors, and it is Earth that resembles a runner passing another by using an inside lane on a turn. Then we increase the distance nightly as our smaller orbit takes us around the sun more quickly.

Not everyone embraced Copernicus's views, especially the leaders of the time. His book was not published until the year he died. But the truth gained hold as more scientists gathered facts. Years of accurate observations by Tycho Brahe (1546–1601) and Johannes Kepler (1571–1630) refined Copernicus's theory. Kepler figured out that each planet's orbit traced an ellipse rather than a circle.

The hunt for new planets is ongoing. The search continues in this solar system beyond Pluto and also around other stars. New discoveries are expected as the technology of telescopes and spacecrafts improves. Whenever planets with Earth-like characteristics are found, **speculation** about them makes people wonder if we will find other life in the universe.

Vocabulary Words

orbited .... traveled around

speculation .... the act of contemplating or thinking about something and forming an opinion

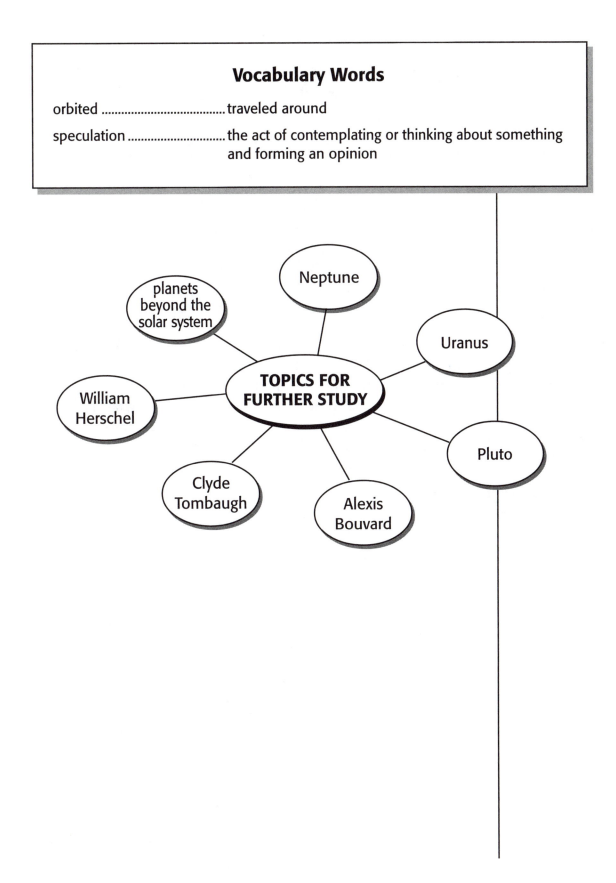

Materials per Team

- meter sticks, measuring tapes, or a trundle wheel

- spheres (pebbles and rocks, even grains of sand) to represent planets in three dimensions

- paper, scissors, and circle-drawing compasses for two-dimensional disks

- calculators (optional)

- large, open space, such as a playground or ballfield

Scale Models

Modeling the Solar System

The scale of the solar system is difficult to comprehend. Constructing scale models can help children compare relative sizes and distances. There are three possible approaches to choose: a scale model of distances from the sun, a scale model of planet diameters, and a combination scale model of distance and size.

All of us find it difficult to grasp great sizes and distances. Shrinking things by many orders of magnitude is a good place to start. Older students can research planet diameters and distances from the sun. Different sources yield different values according to the date printed and the amount of approximation in the calculations. If you want to provide the data, use the table at the top of page 35. Values for distance from the sun are mean values for the planets' orbits, and all numbers are rounded.

Distance

On a playground or field, choose a spot for the sun. The sun can be in the center on a very large field. If you have a smaller area to use, you may have to place the sun at one end and line up the planets.

Table 1: Solar System Data

	Sun	Mercury	Venus	Earth	Mars	Jupiter	Saturn	Uranus	Neptune	Pluto
Distance from sun Earth = 1	—	.4	.7	1	1.5	5.2	9.5	19.2	30.1	39.4
Distance from sun in millions of miles	—	36	67	93	142	486	892	1795	2814	3684
Distance from sun in millions of kilometers	—	58	107	144	227	778	1,427	2,872	4,502	5,894
Diameter Earth = 1	109.2	.4	.95	1	.5	11.2	9.4	4.0	3.9	.2
Diameter in miles	870,000	3,100	7,600	8,000	4,200	89,000	75,000	32,000	30,000	1,500
Diameter in kilometers	1,392,000	4,960	12,160	12,800	6,720	142,400	120,000	51,200	48,000	2,400

Or you can halve the distances in the simulation, although the inner planets can get pretty crowded. Be sure students realize that at any given time, the orbiting planets are in various points in their journey and do not line up. Astronomy magazines publish monthly diagrams of the planets' positions.

Astronomers often use the Earth as a standard of comparison when studying the solar system. Place the Earth 2 meters or yards from the sun. Set the other distances according to the table or student research. Emphasize that these are average distances— Pluto has a particularly eccentric orbit and regained the title of farthest planet in 1999. For a few years before that, Pluto's orbit had brought it closer to the sun than Neptune.

Table 2: Scale Model of Planets' Distance from the Sun

	Sun	Mercury	Venus	Earth	Mars	Jupiter	Saturn	Uranus	Neptune	Pluto
Distance from sun Earth = 2	—	.8	1.4	2	3.0	10.4	19.0	38.4	60.2	78.8

Size

Use Earth as a standard again to begin a size comparison. Cut out a disk with a 2-inch or 5-centimeter diameter. Using metric measures helps here because students' tools for measuring inches probably won't be marked in tenths. Drawing on a playground with chalk can be fun and provides a hands-on measuring experience for the students. Drawing also avoids having to find materials large enough to represent the size of the sun and the giant planets.

Table 3: Scale Model of Planet Sizes

	Sun	Mercury	Venus	Earth	Mars	Jupiter	Saturn	Uranus	Neptune	Pluto
Diameter in inches	218.4	.8	1.90	2	1	22.4	18.8	8.0	7.8	.4
Diameter in centimeters	546	2.0	4.8	5	2.5	56.0	47.0	20.0	19.5	1.0

Distance and Size

Comparing size and distance together is challenging, but the challenge reinforces just how immense the solar system is. Test students' understanding of the problem. Why do the distances grow so huge and the sizes so small in this model? In the other simulations, we set the value for Earth to an arbitrary value, such as two or five. In this exercise, we need to represent both distance and size to the same scale. The Earth's distance from the sun is about 93,000,000 miles, while its diameter is close to 8,000 miles—two very different numbers to fit into one diagram.

In the scale from the distance model in this lesson, each meter equaled approximately 46,750,000 miles. On that scale, the Earth's diameter would be about .00017 meter, or less than two hundredths of a centimeter. And Pluto is one-quarter the size of Earth! So the distance model we made produces planets too small to handle.

Using the scale from the size model in this lesson, each centimeter equaled about 1,595 miles. On that scale, Earth would be more than 586 meters away from the sun. Pluto would be 230 kilometers away, considerably farther than the average schoolyard! Older students can have fun using calculators to figure out where the rest of the planets would be if the size model also included distance.

What we need is a compromise model that shrinks the sizes from the diameters scale and pushes out the positions from the distance scale. Again, you can assign older students to design a simulation, or use the table below if their math skills aren't ready.

Table 4: Combination Distance and Size Scale Model

	Sun	Mercury	Venus	Earth	Mars	Jupiter	Saturn	Uranus	Neptune	Pluto
Diameter in millimeters	580	2	5	5	3	59	50	21	20	1
Distance from sun in meters	—	24	45	60	95	324	594	1,196	1,875	2,456

When setting up the model, it might be helpful to review decimal notation. If you consider the basic metric unit to be 1 meter, point out how small a millimeter is.

meter = 1.0   centimeter = .01   millimeter = .001

Next, see how large a kilometer is.

meter = 1   kilometer = 1,000

Because we need a very small distance in the model to represent a very large distance in the solar system, use millimeters as the unit for size. Make 1 millimeter equal to the smallest part of the model, Pluto's diameter.

1 mm = 2,400 kilometers

Have students scale up to find out what a meter represents in the model.

1 meter = 2,400,000 (2.4 million) kilometers

Even when starting with a planet diameter of 1 millimeter on a scale model, Pluto's average distance from the sun is almost 2.5 kilometers. Very few school yards have the 1.5-mile distance necessary to fit the model on campus!

R E A D I N G:
Cutting It Down to Size

As the year 2000 opened, several spacecraft launched in the 1970s continued their lonely journeys in the outer reaches of the solar system. The Pioneer and Voyager missions explored the giant planets beyond Mars and the **asteroid belt.** Having escaped the gravitational pull of the sun as well as that of the Earth, the travelers continued to send back signals from spectacularly long distances. Because of these machines, scientists are learning more about the region called the **heliosphere**.

The solar system consists of the sun, planets, moons, and other objects that orbit the sun. The heliosphere (*helio* means "sun" in Greek) is the area containing the particles emitted by the sun in a flow called the **solar wind.** This particle flow creates a magnetic field. Where are the boundaries of the heliosphere? What are conditions like beyond the heliosphere? As Pioneer 10 and 11 and Voyager 1 and 2 continue to transmit data to Earth, scientists hope to find answers to these and other questions.

When you make scale models of the solar system, you will find that size and distance can be difficult to represent together. For example, if you fit Pluto's orbit into a schoolyard or field, the model of the planet itself will be very tiny. But when you represent planet sizes with objects big enough to measure and compare, the outer planets will need to be placed well off the school grounds. Try using a map of your local area and plotting a scale model solar system on it. That will help you appreciate how far Pioneer and Voyager have traveled. Thanks to them, we may soon be able to include the heliosphere on our scale model.

Since 1930, people have known about nine planets in our solar system; in order, from the sun outward, they are Mercury, Venus, Earth, Mars, Jupiter, Saturn, Uranus, Neptune, and

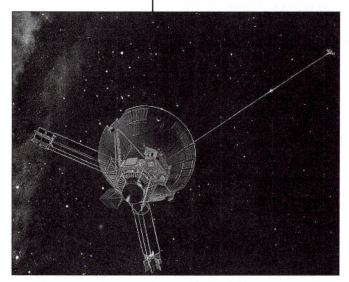

Pioneer spacecraft (courtesy of NASA)

Pluto. The orbits of Neptune and Pluto do not actually cross but each planet can claim the title of "farthest planet from the sun" at some time during its orbit.

Because Pluto is usually the most remote, the order of planets can be abbreviated M V E M J S U N P. Do you like **mnemonics**? A well known sentence reads, "<u>M</u>y <u>V</u>ery <u>E</u>xcellent <u>M</u>other <u>J</u>ust <u>S</u>howed <u>U</u>s <u>N</u>ine <u>P</u>lanets." Can you make up another sentence to help people remember the order of the planets? What will be the names of new planets discovered beyond the orbit of Pluto?

Since the 1930s, astronomers have not only used light waves but also radio waves to observe space. Radio signals have revealed the existence of objects such as **pulsars** and **quasars.** They were unknown until the mid-twentieth century and have expanded our ideas about the scope of the universe. Vehicles traveling away from Earth as well as orbiting telescopes in space, such as the Hubble Telescope, continue to improve scientists' views into the universe. These tools improve our understanding of the solar system, our neighborhood in space.

Hubble Space Telescope (courtesy of NASA)

Vocabulary Words

asteroid belt .... band of small rocky objects orbiting the sun between the orbits of Mars and Jupiter

heliosphere .... the vast magnetic bubble surrounding the solar system, the solar wind, and the magnetic field around the sun

mnemonics .... devices, symbols, reminders, and so on, that can be used to help remember something

pulsar .... a source of radio energy from space, believed to be a rotating neutron star

quasar .... quasi-stellar object; small but powerful source of energy

solar wind .... atoms and ions blowing out from the sun through the solar system

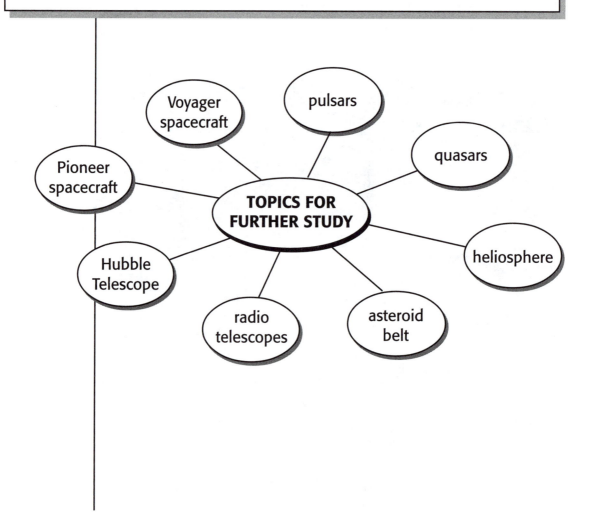

Comets

Modeling Distant Travelers

Materials per Team

- fan to move air— either a safe household unit or small battery- powered model

- Styrofoam spheres and pencils, or tennis balls attached to string with push pins

- thin paper or ribbon streamers

- tape

- photos of comets

We Earthlings view comets with awe. They visit our neighbor- hood infrequently, arriving from very distant regions. They travel across the sky in paths differing greatly from the moon, planets, and stars. A comet's most striking characteristic is probably its tail, a cone-shaped streak extending from the main body, or nucleus, of the comet. Here, students will build their own comets.

Teams of students can build comets in several ways. Figuring out how to do it can be part of the challenge, or you can suggest a series of steps. Have students use a Styrofoam ball and stick a pencil into it for a handle. Or, they can stick a push pin into a tennis ball or other soft sphere and tie a string to the pin. For the tail, they can glue or tape light streamers of paper or ribbon onto the sphere.

Halley's comet (courtesy of NASA)

41

The tail consists of particles pushed away from the comet's nucleus by solar energy. Because solar wind travels outward, the tails of comets always point away from the sun. Students might confuse the direction of motion and the position of the tail. When a comet is approaching the sun, the tail will be "behind" the comet, similar to the tail of an animal that is moving. After the comet rounds the sun and heads back to the outer reaches of the solar system, the tail will be in "front" of the comet, seeming to lead the way. Modeling comets can be helpful.

To simulate solar wind, use a safe fan. Remind students that solar wind consists of gases from the sun's atmosphere flowing away into space. Keep the fan in one place while students walk their spheres around it. Aiming the airflow at the "comet" when it is at any position pushes the tail away from the "sun," no matter which direction the student is traveling. The farther from the sun, the less energy there is to affect the comet, and the tail will be smaller.

READING:
Dirty Snowballs

Through thousands of years of astronomy, people discovered nine planets orbiting the sun. Some of the planets have moons orbiting them, and some are circled by rings of smaller objects. Between Mars and Jupiter lies an asteroid belt, a region of orbiting objects too small to be considered planets.

Another type of visitor makes an occasional appearance in our neighborhood of the solar system—**comets.** A comet looks like a fuzzy star and travels in an elliptical path. But while the ellipse a planet travels is close to circular, a comet's ellipse is much more flattened. The sun is one of the focal points, and the other focal point may be far out in space. One complete orbit around the sun may take millions of years.

Comets develop tails as they near the sun. The tail always points away from the sun as seen from the main part, or nucleus, of the comet. Scientists sometimes describe comets as "dirty snowballs" made up of frozen gases, dust, and ice. (Fred Whipple, 1906–2004, first used that phrase in 1949.) Larger chunks similar to the rocky material that make up **meteors** may be present also. Near the sun, some of the ice evaporates, leaving particles behind. The energy of the sun in the form of heat and **solar wind** pushes these particles into a fan-shaped tail.

Solar wind consists of gases streaming out into space away from the sun. These gases may travel many millions of miles and pass Earth at very high speeds.

Where do comets come from? In 1950, Jan Heindrich Oort (1900–1992) theorized that beyond Pluto's orbit there is a huge cloud of material. Comets form when parts of this cloud are dislodged and are pulled toward the sun.

Edmond Halley (1656–1742) predicted the return of a comet he and others observed in 1682. Halley claimed it was the same comet that had been reappearing about every seventy-seven years and would therefore be back around 1758. People had reported seeing this comet as far back as 2400 B.C.

Although he was not alive to see it return, his prediction proved correct and the comet was later named for him. He had helped convince scientists that comets were part of the solar system and traveled in elliptical orbits.

Earlier astronomers, including stargazers from ancient civilizations and Tycho Brahe (1546–1601), observed comets and wondered about these deep space travelers. Caroline Herschel (1750–1848) was one of the best discoverers of comets ever—by 1797, she had found eight in an eleven-year span. In 1866, William Huggins (1824–1910) studied the **spectrum** emitted by a comet and its tail. This process began to reveal its chemical composition. Huggins had studied the spectra (plural of *spectrum*) of stars and was experienced in determining the presence of different elements.

Even in modern times, the appearance of a beautiful comet in the dark, starry sky makes us appreciate our connection to the vastness of the universe. Learning about comets continues. Space vehicles are able to record closer and closer views of comets. In 2004, the spacecraft Stardust passed within hundreds of kilometers of a comet, capturing samples of material streaming into space. In 2005, spacecraft Deep Impact sent out a probe that crashed into another comet. Scientists believe that the data collected and the dust and gas they examine will help them understand how **chemical elements** have formed in space. Perhaps there will be new clues about the "Big Bang" theory of how the universe was formed.

You can build model comets and learn about the different parts. Keep up with the science news to learn about new discoveries. And be sure to greet the next comet that comes visiting—it's had a long journey.

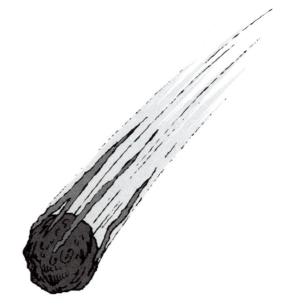

Vocabulary Words

chemical .... relating to chemistry, having to do with the structure and properties of matter; also a term for a substance used in a chemical reaction or process

comet .... small, icy body that orbits the sun

element .... substance composed of one type of atom

meteor .... small object traveling through space

solar wind .... atoms and ions blowing from the sun outward through the solar system

spectrum .... sequence or range of energy by wavelength

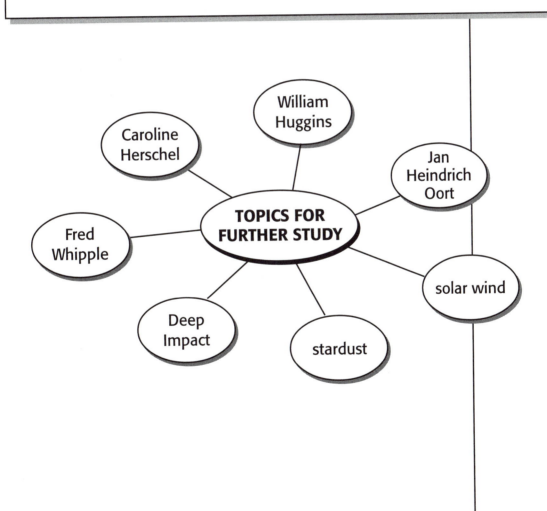

CHAPTER 2
Earth History

TIME LINE

Year	Notable Event
500s B.C.	Xenophanes of Greece discovered fossilized sea creatures on mountains and reasoned that the area must have been underwater at some time.
1620	Francis Bacon noted the similarities in coastlines on opposite sides of the Atlantic Ocean.
1650	Archbishop James Ussher calculated the beginning of the Earth to have occurred in 4004 B.C.
1669	Nicolaus Steno studied the layers of Earth and the fossils they contained.
1774	Abraham Werner published a book about minerals and argued that Earth layers formed as a result of ancient sea sediments.
1785	James Hutton claimed that modern Earth processes are the same as those that formed the existing surface features, a theory known as *uniformitarianism.*
1833	Charles Lyell published a book that argued convincingly that the Earth is many millions of years old.
1912	Alfred Wegener proposed his theory of continental drift.
1915	Wegener described Pangaea, a supercontinent from ancient times.
1928	Arthur Holmes hypothesized that heat within the Earth could be driving continental drift.
1960	Harry Hess explained his theory of seafloor spreading.
1980	Walter and Luis Alvarez theorized that a catastrophe like a meteorite strike caused the extinctions and climate changes that occurred sixty-five million years ago.

Materials per Team

- rolls of paper (adding machine tape works well)
- meter sticks or measuring tapes
- cardboard tubes from wrapping paper rolls
- calculators

Making Time Lines

Relating Time to Distance

The scale of geologic time is awe-inspiring. The huge numbers overwhelm adults, and for children, the vastness of time can be unimaginable. In this activity, students will create models representing time with lengths of common materials. Using rolls of paper to make a series of time lines can give students a feeling for how truly old the Earth is.

Building time lines nicely integrates math and science, provides practice in scale modeling and analogies, and reduces inconceivably large numbers to more understandable scales. This activity provides instructions for three scale models.

Remember that numbers are rounded and geological time estimates are based on many assumptions. For example, the fossil record used by scientists contains gaps, and the farther back in time we look, the hazier evidence can be. The most widely accepted age of the Earth is 4.6 billion years. Other ways to express this number are 4,600,000,000, 4.6×10^9, and 4,600 million. Gauge your students' understanding of place value and determine how best to represent large numbers.

Model 1

Imagine the history of the Earth as a ride up an elevator in a ninety-two-story building. Have students use tubes from wrapping paper rolls or other tall materials to construct scale models, or stand a meter stick up for a quick "skyscraper." Each story or floor represents about 50,000,000 (50 million) years. Each twenty floors equals about a billion years. Using that information, older students can work independently or as teams to research Earth history and place the events on their building.

A chart to use with younger students is shown on page 49. Be sure to point out how math is used to create the analogy—learning proportion is a useful skill.

Event	Millions of Years Ago	Floor No.
Earth forms	4,600	ground (1st)
Origin of first life	4,000	12th
Evidence of life from fossils	3,000	32nd
Buildup of oxygen	2,800–2,000	36th–52nd
Multicelled organisms	600–550	80th–81st
Early fish	510	82nd
Age of dinosaurs	290–65	86th–91st
Humanlike primates	5	92nd (30 cm/1 ft from ceiling)
Homo sapiens	1	92nd (10 cm/4 in. from ceiling)
Columbus sails to America	.0005	92nd (.005 cm/.002 in. from ceiling)

The scale is approximately 15 ft/story in a real building:

▶ 30 cm/12 in. equals about 3.3 million years

▶ 2.5 cm/1 in. equals about 278,000 years

Model 2

Drawing a time line on the playground can be fun, or find another distance familiar to your students. Here's a simplified set of measurements using the following scale:

> 1 centimeter = 10 million years, or
> 1 inch = 25 million years

Numbers are rounded for simplicity, using the ratio 1 inch = 2.5 centimeters.

Rolls of adding machine paper are useful for these scales—students can draw on them and the paper can be attached to a wall or bulletin board.

Length in Centimeters	Length in Inches	Process Occurring
100.0	40.0	Earth cools for a billion years
325.0	130.0	life evolves to age of dinosaurs (3.5 billion to 225 million years ago)
15.0	6.0	age of dinosaurs (225 to 65 million years ago)
7.5	3.0	mammals developed but before humans (65 to 5 million years ago)
0.5	0.2	humans evolve from primates (about 5 million years)

Model 3

Here's a model based on time rather than length. Imagine the history of the Earth compressed into 1 year. Use calculators to help older students convert 4,600,000,000 into 365 days. The ratio works out to about 12,602,739 years for each calendar day, and about 525,114 years per hour. Each minute in our simulated year stands for about 8,752 years of Earth history, and every second represents 146 years. For younger students, round off the numbers.

Event or Process	Millions of Years Before Present Time	Calendar Date
Earth forms	4,600	January 1
Origin of life	4,000	February 15–20
Evidence of fossils	3,000	April 5–10
Buildup of oxygen	2,800–2,000	April 21–25
Multicelled organisms	600–550	November 10–20
Early fish	510	November 25
Dinosaurs appeared	225	December 14
Dinosaur extinction	65	around Christmas
Historical civilizations	.005	an hour or two before midnight
Columbus's journey	.0005	within the last 3 seconds of the year

What other models can students invent? Older students can make up their own analogies and compute. Younger students can create graphs, diagrams, and artwork to accompany the time lines and display them in common areas of the school.

READING:
How Old Is the Earth?

People have always wondered how old the Earth is and how it got its start. **Creation stories** abound in most cultures. As scientific knowledge has grown over time, so has our ability to understand the life story of our planet.

Many clues to the history of the Earth lie within its rocks. The Greeks saw **fossils** of sea creatures high in the mountains and may have recognized them as being animals from **antiquity.** Other cultures told of great floods or of gods forming the Earth into its present shape. Volcanoes and earthquakes gave indications of awesome forces within the Earth.

Around 1650, Archbishop James Ussher (1581–1656) used the Bible and the generations detailed in it to trace history back to the Creation. He calculated the date of creation as October 26, 4004 B.C. In the following centuries, many scientists performed experiments to determine the Earth's origins. In France, Comte de Buffon (1707–1788) heated iron in his laboratory and measured its cooling rate. Working with the theory that Earth was once molten rock and has cooled to its current state, he **extrapolated** the values of cooling iron to find the cooling rate for the Earth. Buffon arrived at an age of seventy-five thousand years for the Earth, estimating it to be more than seventy thousand years older than the Archbishop's calculation.

William Thomson (1824–1907), later known as Lord Kelvin, also used the theory of a once molten Earth cooling to its present state in order to estimate the age of the Earth. He calculated the figure to be between twenty million and a hundred million years. But the cooling method had a major problem. **Radioactive** rocks emit energy and the Earth is still producing heat, so we can't assume a measure of steady cooling over time. Thus, Lord Kelvin's theory was disproved.

Nicholas Steno (1638–1686), an early discoverer of fossils, described layers of geological material (rocks), which are continually being laid down and eroded, in the present as they were in the past. Later scientists were able to use the fossils contained in the rock layers as evidence for many theories about the history of the Earth.

Palm frond fossil in Green River Shale, Wyoming (courtesy of The Virtual Fossil Museum)

From *Science Giants: Earth and Space* © Good Year Books. This page may be reproduced for classroom use only by the actual purchaser of the book. www.goodyearbooks.com

The man generally considered to be the first geologist, James Hutton (1726–1797), pushed the estimate of the Earth's age up into the millions. Hutton advanced several principles that sent Earth Science on its way to joining the other experimental sciences. Hutton believed in a theory called **uniformitarianism.** He supposed that the processes we observe today are similar to those that have occurred throughout Earth's history. These processes work slowly, so Hutton reasoned that the Earth is very old.

Charles Bonnet (1720–1793) described the occurrence of floods, volcanoes, earthquakes, and other violent natural acts that caused changes in the Earth's features. Bonnet and others argued that this process, called **catastrophism,** affected organisms so strongly that they evolved into new species.

Georges Cuvier (1769–1832) classified fossils and living organisms according to the **Linnaean classification system** of species and broader categories. By recognizing that animals preserved as fossils could be ancient ancestors of modern creatures, Cuvier helped advance the argument that the Earth is very old. He also agreed with Bonnet about ancient natural catastrophes changing the Earth.

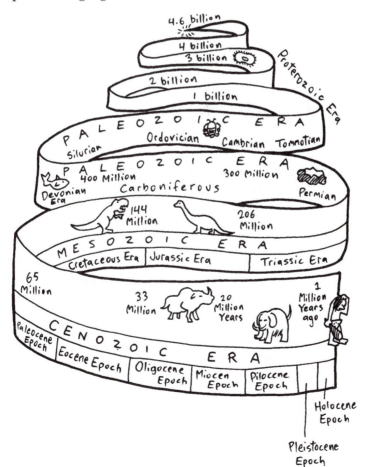

Some of the most persuasive arguments for an ancient Earth came from Charles Lyell (1797–1875). Lyell pointed out changes in the Earth's crust that required enormous stretches of time to take place. Charles Darwin (1809–1882) agreed with Lyell. Darwin built his **evolution theory** using the background of an Earth with a long history.

In 1980, Walter Alvarez (b. 1940) and his father Luis Alvarez (1911–1988) brought catastrophism to the forefront of Earth science. They theorized that a meteorite struck Earth and caused the extinction of dinosaurs and other great changes sixty-five million years ago.

By 1900, discoveries about the atom brought geologists powerful tools for finding the age of the Earth's rocks and there is now general agreement that the Earth is very old. **Radiometric dating** calculates the age of minerals by measuring the concentration of radioactive **elements** present. The time it takes 50 percent of one element's atoms to change to another element (or a variety of the same element) is called its **half-life.** Often, by measuring how much of the original element is present, scientists can calculate the age of the rock. By the late twentieth century, estimates of the age of the Earth had reached about 4.6 billion years.

Vocabulary Words

antiquity	ancient times
catastrophism	the theory that the surface of the Earth was formed by a series of catastrophic events, such as floods and volcanic eruptions
creation story	tale told to explain the formation of the Earth and other natural phenomena
element	substance composed of one type of atom
evolution theory	the theory that genetic changes from generation to generation over time cause species to change gradually
extrapolated	carried calculations further
fossil	the remains of ancient organisms

Vocabulary Words *(continued)*

half-life .... time period over which half the amount of a radioactive element will decay

Linnaean
classification system .... system for categorizing organisms. Using this system, scientists identify each species with a two-part name that reflects a general and specific group

radioactive .... describes material that emits radiation from the nuclei (plural of *nucleus*) of its atoms

radiometric dating .... method of determining the age of ancient material. Scientists measure the ratio of radioactive elements remaining in a sample and compare it to elements formed as the radioactive material decays.

uniformitarianism .... theory that states that the processes occurring on Earth now are similar to those that affected the Earth in the past

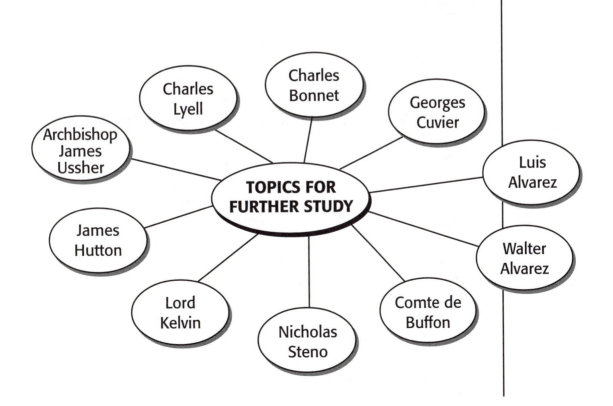

Materials per Team

- laboratory thermometers
- hot water
- cups
- data recording sheets
- graph paper

Cooling Rates

How Things Cool

In this activity, students will record and graph the temperature of hot water as it cools over time. Before scientists understood that some elements in the Earth were radioactive and emitted energy, cooling rates were used to estimate the age of the Earth.

You might find the thermometers you need for this activity in a science teacher's lab or you can purchase them from a science supply catalogue (they are usually inexpensive). Be sure the thermometer can withstand the temperatures you plan to measure.

Note: *Do not use household air temperature thermometers. They can break and become a safety hazard.*

Before doing the experiment, explain the procedure and safety rules. Students will be working with hot water and need to be very careful not to spill it. How long will it take a cup of hot water to cool? Give each student two copies of the blank graph on page 58. On one graph, ask them to predict and draw what they think a graph of the water temperature over time will look like. Then have student teams do the experiment. Students should then fill in the other graph with their findings. Have them compare the actual data to their predictions. (Students can also use one graph, but chart predictions and actual data in different colors.)

Fill several cups with hot tap water or water that you have heated. The older and more reliable students are, the hotter the water you can use. Using boiling water with older students helps them learn that 100° Celsius is a limit for water under usual circumstances. Measuring water that has been poured from a tea pot just after boiling will measure less than 100° Celsius because the heat source has been removed and it will cool a degree or two immediately.

Have students place a sturdy thermometer in each cup and record the temperature. Do this quickly as the temperature drops fast. Record the temperatures at one-minute intervals for at least twenty minutes. After twenty minutes, students can take readings at longer time intervals.

Compare the results against student predictions by graphing the cooling curves. Did they differ? Why or why not?

Most students will have drawn a straight line for their prediction. The actual experimental data will be a curve, steep at first and then flattening as it approaches room temperature. The number of degrees of cooling is not the same each minute. The gap between the water temperature and the room temperature drives the rate of cooling. The gap is large at first, so the cooling curve is steeper. As the gap closes, the curve flattens.

Try the experiment with water that is cooled below room temperature and graph the warming curve. How does that curve compare to a cooling curve?

Lord Kelvin tried to determine the age of the Earth by calculating how long it would have taken molten rock to cool. His estimate of the Earth's age was far too short. He also did not factor in the continuing heating of the Earth due to the energy released by radioactive minerals. When students perform the activity on the cooling rate of water, they will find that several variables affect the cooling rates in their experiment, too. Have them brainstorm factors that would slow or quicken cooling of a hot drink—insulating properties of the cup, use of a cover, surface area of the liquid, and so on.

Activity Graph

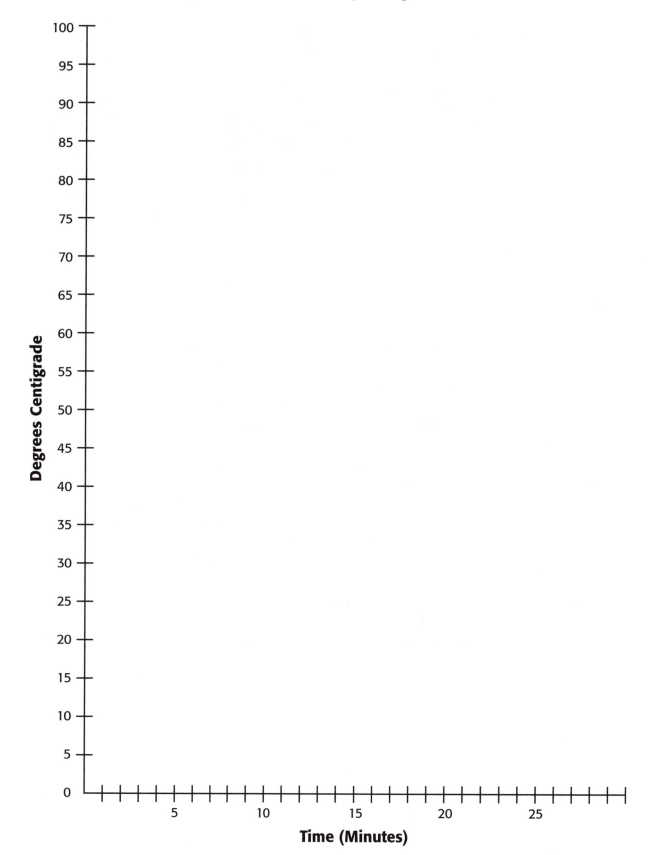

Degrees Centigrade

Time (Minutes)

READING:
Cooling Off

By the early 1800s, most scientists agreed that some rock is formed from **magma,** which is what molten rock is called when it is underground. Volcanoes can be seen sending out **lava,** molten rock that is on the Earth's surface. Lava cools and hardens rapidly once it is exposed to air and/or water.

English scientist William Thomson (1824–1907), who became Lord Kelvin, thought he could use the cooling rate method to determine an accurate age for the Earth. He melted rocks in his laboratory and recorded their cooling rates. He adjusted the time for a quantity of rock the size of the Earth and estimated a cooling time in the tens of millions of years.

Lord Kelvin was using the laws of thermodynamics, the study of heat and other forms of energy. The laws of thermodynamics help explain many scientific principles. The first law says that in a closed system, the amount of energy is constant. When you measure the temperature of hot water in a cup over time, you realize its heat energy is decreasing. But where does the heat go?

According to the second law of **thermodynamics,** the heat always moves from warmer places to cooler ones, in this case from the hot water to the room-temperature air. The heat in the water has not disappeared—it has moved.

Kelvin succeeded in pushing back the time line of Earth history, but not far enough. He didn't know that the Earth contains some rocks that actually create heat. **Radioactive elements** in those rocks are decaying and emitting tiny particles, as matter is converting to energy. Also, the Earth is not a closed system—the sun's rays heat the surface of the Earth and affect its temperature.

Lord Kelvin added greatly to the understanding of thermo-dynamics. He devised a temperature scale that is named after him. The Kelvin scale includes **absolute zero,** a condition in which there is no heat energy.

Plate tectonics theories since Kelvin's time have taught us that the interior of the Earth is a dynamic, active system. Many of the geologic processes we experience on the surface are powered by the actions occurring beneath the surface and under the seas. Heat energy within the Earth powers plate tectonics.

Cooling rates alone are not enough to determine the age of the Earth. When you do a cooling experiment in your classroom, you see that even a container of water is subject to many variables. A complex system like the Earth's layers and crust will not yield a simple formula for cooling. See if you can find estimates of the temperatures at different levels beneath the Earth's surface.

An erupting volcano (photograph by J.D. Griggs, courtesy of U.S. Department of the Interior, U.S. Geological Survey)

Vocabulary Words

absolute zero	temperature at which particles have no heat energy, calculated to be about 273° C
element	substance composed of one type of atom
lava	molten rock that reaches the surface of the Earth
magma	molten rock below the Earth's surface
plate tectonics theory	theory that states that the movement of plates below the Earth's surface drives the geological processes on the surface
radioactive	describes material that emits radiation from the nuclei (plural of *nucleus*) of its atoms
thermodynamics	the study of the relationship between heat and other forms of energy

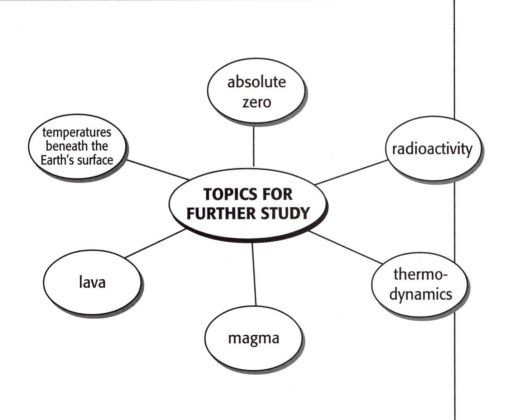

Materials per Team

- plaster of Paris
- shells, plant materials or small bones
- sturdy disposable plates or containers
- Vaseline® or mineral oil
- modeling clay

Fossils

Making Model Fossils

Fossils form when the remains of living creatures are buried in sediment that hardens to rock. The process occurs over a long period of time. Using plaster of Paris, students can make impressions of shells, leaves, and bones to simulate fossils. Try each of these methods in advance to see which will work best for your students.

Method 1

To start, have students mix the plaster of Paris according to directions on the container. They can then pour it onto a sturdy plate or other base that will hold the hardened plaster. Have all plant and animal material at hand as the plaster dries quickly. Have students coat the specimen with Vaseline or oil and press gently into the plaster. Allow the plaster to dry and peel off the specimen. The remaining impression represents a fossil of the once-living organism.

Method 2

Producing a cast is another way to make a fossil. Have students press the object being fossilized into modeling clay. After they remove the object, it will leave an impression. They can then rub the impression, or mold, with Vaseline or oil and carefully pour plaster of Paris into the mold. After the plaster sets, they can remove the model fossil.

Method 3

Pressing the animal or plant part into the plaster of Paris and letting it set is a third way to do this activity. Students can put clay around the object after the plaster has hardened. Pour more plaster over the fossil and let that set. When they separate the two halves, they'll have a cast of the fossil.

Real fossils are produced in sedimentary rock. Sedimentary rock forms in layers that can cover and preserve dead organisms. Organic material that is buried decomposes more slowly than that in open air. Minerals can gradually take the place and shape of the once-living cells. The minerals harden into rock, creating a fossil representation of the ancient organism.

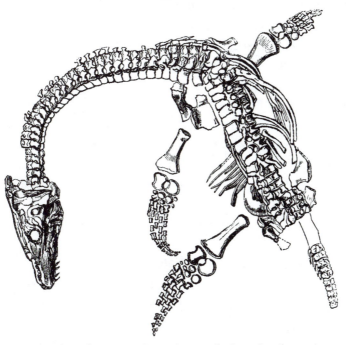

Drawing of a Mesozoic marine reptile from fossil remains

R E A D I N G:
Preserved in Stone

Fossils are the preserved forms of organisms that died long ago. If a specimen is buried quickly, its rate of **decay** can be slow enough for **minerals** to accumulate and take the place of its **cells.** People have found fossils for centuries. However, the significance of fossils as markers on time lines of Earth history is fairly recent.

Fossils have provided many important clues for **geologists.** Scientists can try to estimate the age of a rock layer by studying the fossil remains of the plants and animals that lived when the layer was forming. But first, people had to understand how rock layers accumulated.

Sometimes fossils have led scientists to conclusions that later discoveries disprove or dispute. Xenophanes (570–475 B.C.), a scholar from the ancient Greek world, wrote of discovering sea fossils on mountains and reasoned that water must have covered the Earth in ancient times. Modern scientists explain sea fossils at high elevations as the result of uplift forces in the Earth. Aristotle (384–322 B.C.), the ancient Greek scientist, mentioned fossils in his book *Meteorology*. But he thought fossils were produced within the Earth and then rose to the surface.

In 1669, Nicolaus Steno (1638–1686) proposed the theory of **superposition.** He reasoned that as rock layers are deposited, the oldest layers, or strata, are on the bottom and the newest ones on the top.

William Smith (1769–1839) learned from his experiences and discoveries building canals. Smith found that similar layers of rock contained similar fossils as he worked in different parts of Great Britain. He matched strata (rock layers) in widespread areas of England by identifying the age of rock layers through the fossils in them. He could tell whether layers of rock in different locations were the same age by comparing their fossil records.

Georges Cuvier (1769–1832) of France also published his ideas about fossils being keys to the relative age of rock strata. Cuvier explained that the fossils buried in rock layers lived during the time the layers were forming. Geologists learned to hunt for layers of **coal** by identifying the types of fossils found nearby.

By the middle of the nineteenth century, lots of people were excited about fossils because they are a guide to the past. Richard Owen (1804–1892) made up the word **dinosaurs.** Fossil specimens of these real-life prehistoric monsters were put on public display. In the twentieth century, fossils helped prove the idea that the continents have moved over time— similar fossils were discovered in South America and Africa. These continents, now separated by the Atlantic Ocean, were together at one time. Alfred Wegener (1880–1930) proposed the theory of **continental drift** in the early twentieth century, but it was not until the 1960s that most geologists accepted it.

Every year, surprising or important new fossil finds are discovered around the world. Be sure to keep a lookout in the science news for recent developments.

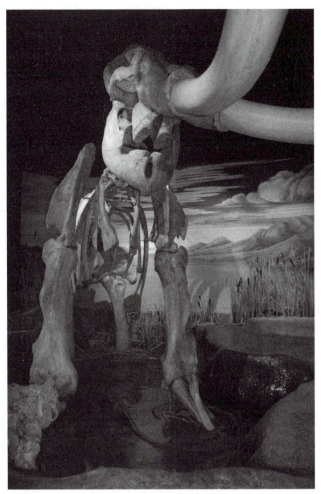

Black Rock Mammoth skeleton
(courtesy of Nevada State Museum, Carson City, Nevada)

Vocabulary Words

cell .... the smallest, microscopic-sized unit of organisms

coal .... the hardened remains of ancient plants, metamorphosed into a hot, burning fuel

continental drift .... the movement of continents relative to each other

decay .... break down into parts

dinosaur .... word meaning "monstrous lizard," a general name for a variety of extinct reptiles that lived more than sixty-five million years ago

geologist .... scientist who studies the history and structure of the Earth

mineral .... naturally occurring solid substance with a specific chemical composition and crystal structure. Minerals are inorganic, which means they do not come from living things.

superposition .... theory that states that layers closer to Earth's surface are younger than those layers beneath them, except in the case of a disturbance

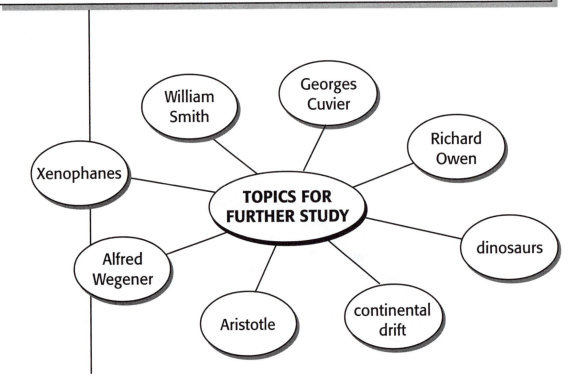

Mountain Building

How Mountains Grow

Paper and clay offer a simple way to demonstrate mountain building. Have students gently but steadily push from both ends of a sheet of paper, or a flattened piece of clay, toward the center. Ripples and bumps of many shapes will push up along the surface. Explain that one current example of a mountain building process is India moving into the rest of Asia.

To simulate mountain activity at plate boundaries, use two pieces of cardboard or oaktag paper. Slide the two pieces toward each other, pushing from the back. One piece will eventually slip under the other, with lots of friction and folding on the way. This simulates the case in which one tectonic plate carrying a continent rides up over another carrying an oceanic basin. Mountains can arise on the continent along with lots of geological action. Magma rises toward the surface, heated by the friction of one plate diving under the other in a process called *subduction*. The Andes Mountains overlooking the west coast of South America have formed in this way.

Materials per Team
- paper
- modeling clay

R E A D I N G:
The Changing Earth

Science often tackles big questions. One of the biggest of all has been "How did the Earth get its form?" Big questions like that usually don't have easy answers.

Earth scientists work like detectives. They hunt for clues and then try to interpret facts from the information they can find. But different people can read the same clues in different ways. Over the last three or four centuries, scientists have developed amazing stories about the Earth's history. When more information is discovered, stories might have to change to fit the facts. As in other fields, change in Earth science often comes as a result of conflicting viewpoints being argued and tested.

James Hutton (1726–1797) is considered one of the first geologists. Hutton was called a Plutonist because of his views on Earth history. **Plutonists** believed that rocks with crystal structures are born *within* the Earth. The name comes from Pluto, Roman god of the Underworld.

Hutton and other Plutonists believed that as volcanic lava cools, new rock forms. We now know this cooling and crystalizing process can take place underground as well. Some solid rock forms below the Earth's surface. Hutton and other Plutonists considered heat energy to be the primary cause of change to the Earth's surface.

Some eighteenth-century scientists disagreed with Hutton. They believed rocks formed from the settling of chemicals in ancient oceans. These **Neptunists,** named after Neptune, Roman god of the sea, felt that the Earth would change no further. Abraham Werner (1750–1817) was one of the major proponents of Neptunism. Werner thought a great **deluge,** or rain, had covered the entire Earth long ago. When the water subsided, the rock formations were laid down.

By the early 1800s, most scientists agreed with Hutton. They recognized **magma,** or underground molten rock, as a major source of rock. James Hall (1761–1832) melted rock in a laboratory and observed that it crystallized as it cooled.

The great heat energy of the Earth keeps the crust very active. Giant plates slowly move about the surface of the Earth, carrying continents and oceans. When one of these **tectonic plates** carrying a continent rides up over another carrying an ocean basin, mountains arise on the continent. Magma rises toward the surface, heated by the friction of one plate diving under the other, a process called **subduction.** The Andes Mountains overlooking the west coast of South America formed in this way.

Volcanic mountains arise over the site of other plate collisions. The Cascade Mountains of the northwest United States have active volcanic eruptions caused by the friction of plates coming together. Look at a map of earthquakes and volcanoes and you will see where boundaries of plates collide. Can you find the part of the Earth called the "ring of fire"?

Rocky Mountain National Park (photograph by W.T. Lee, U.S. Geological Survey)

Vocabulary Words

deluge ....a great rain or flood

magma ....molten rock below the Earth's surface

Neptunist ....one who believed that great flooding shaped the surface of the Earth

Plutonist ....one who believed that heat formed rocks and shaped the Earth

subduction ....process by which a plate on the ocean floor slides beneath another plate as the two collide

tectonic plates ....large segments of the Earth's layer called the lithosphere that move around, affecting the surface configuration of the continents, oceans, and other features

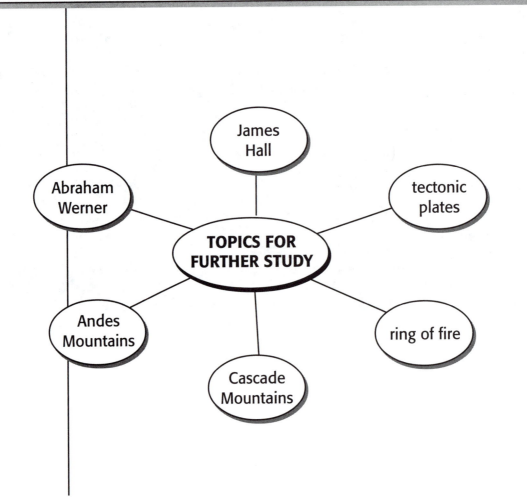

Continents

The Restless Earth

The Earth is a dynamic planet with an active and changing surface. Over the vast periods of Earth history, continents have moved and oceans have formed and disappeared. Geologists have theorized that plates moving below the surface of the Earth drive the changing configuration of the continents and oceans. In this activity, students will use maps to manipulate continents and represent ancient configurations of the world.

Start this activity by providing students with two copies of page 73, the outline maps of the continents. Have them cut out two sets of continents and set aside one set. Then ask them to use a reference map (page 72—copy at approximately 150% of current size) to assemble Pangaea from one set of continents. Have teams discuss the placement of each continent before gluing anything in place.

Use the second set of continents to build the world as it is arranged today. Note that Antarctica is drawn so it can be placed on a flat map of the world. Be sure students consult a globe and notice the actual shape of the continent. Challenge older students to set the continents in place without looking at a map.

Before gluing down continents in their current configuration, have students check current plate tectonics movements. What might the Earth look like in the far-off future? Students can calculate how further changes over long periods of time will occur if current plate movements continue, and they can move their cut-out continents accordingly. Here are some examples:

- The mid-oceanic spreading between Europe and North America moves at about 2 centimeters per year.
- The Eastern Pacific Ocean is widening at a rate of about 10 centimeters per year off the coast of South America.
- Two plates sliding past each other causing California's San Andreas fault are moving about 5 centimeters per year in opposite directions.

Materials per Team

- two copies of page 73, outline maps of the Earth's continents
- simple map or template of the Earth
- copy of the map of Pangaea, the supercontinent, on page 72 at approximately 150% of current size
- scissors
- paper
- glue

Encourage students to do the math and see how much wider the Atlantic Ocean would be at its current pace of spreading. The distances seem small by our time scale, but geologic time is vast. Every hundred years, the Atlantic is about 2 meters wider. After a thousand years, the change is 20 meters—still not too significant. But over a million years, the distance is 20 kilometers, or more than 8 miles. Given how old the planet is, and with continents and oceans moving positions continuously, it makes sense that maps of pre-historic Earth will look very different from our familiar world map.

Conclude the activity by having students compare the map of Pangaea and the twenty-first-century map.

From *Science Giants: Earth and Space* © Good Year Books. This page may be reproduced for classroom use only by the actual purchaser of the book. www.goodyearbooks.com

READING:

Putting the Pieces Together

A new revolution in thinking about the age of the Earth greeted the twentieth century. How long had the Earth looked the way it does? Alfred Wegener (1880–1930), a German scientist, announced his revolutionary theory of **continental drift** in 1912. The continents and oceans had not always occupied their current positions, Wegener claimed, and are in fact, in motion.

Several pieces of strong evidence supported Wegener and the case grew stronger as the century progressed:

- The continents look like puzzle pieces. Look at a map of the world and you will clearly see this.
- Similar rocks and fossils are found on continents now widely separated. Over time they may have drifted apart, but it is apparent to scientists that some animals who lived together in the same region are now in different parts of the world.
- Plant and animal fossils indicate radically different climates in years past. Regions that now experience extreme cold have fossils of tropical organisms.

Arthur Holmes (1890–1965) suggested a mechanism for continental drift. Holmes explained that heat within the Earth could provide the energy to move the giant landmasses.

Harry Hess (1906–1969) demonstrated that the seafloor is spreading at certain points in the oceans. New **crust** is being produced from **rifts,** or splits, in the ocean floor. This helped scientists develop the **plate tectonics theory.** The Earth's crust is now believed to be composed of plates. The plates move slowly, driven by the formation and spreading of new crust emerging from beneath the surface of the Earth.

When new rock forms from **lava, minerals** affected by **magnetism** line up according to the magnetic poles of the Earth. The minerals "freeze," or solidify, in that pattern.

The magnetic record supports Wegener's theory of continental drift. The pattern can tell scientists where the poles were in relation to the rock when it formed. The poles have both reversed and moved around the globe. This "polar wander" movement can be traced using the magnetic patterns in the rocks on the continents. The pattern reveals that all the continents were joined together at one time as a supercontinent, Pangaea. The continents have since drifted apart to new configurations.

Putting all of these hypotheses together extended the estimate of the age of the Earth considerably. The slow process of **erosion** needs a vast number of years to uncover rocks that have **crystallized** within the Earth. The movement caused by plate tectonics requires millions of years to create oceans, mountain ranges, and other geological features.

Check into current plate tectonic movements. What might the Earth look like in the far distant future? Although plate movement is slow by our standards, the Earth's continents move at a different pace from us. Small movements occurring over long periods of time create major changes.

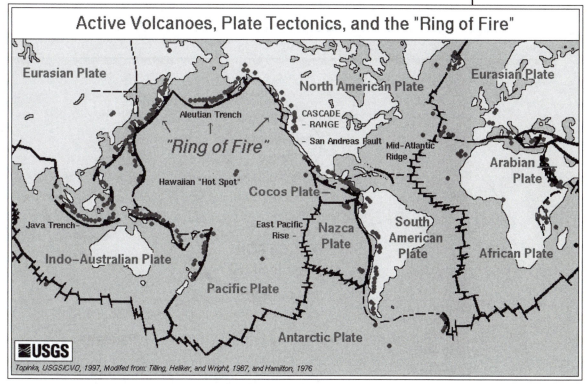

A map of the Earth's plates (courtesy of U.S. Geological Survey)

Vocabulary Words

continental drift .... the movement of continents relative to each other

crust .... a layer of the Earth, the outermost layer of the lithosphere

crystallized .... having formed crystals

erosion .... process by which rock and soil are loosened and carried away

lava .... molten rock that reaches the surface of the Earth

magnetism .... having the properties of a magnet

mineral .... naturally occurring solid substance with a specific chemical composition and crystal structure. Minerals are inorganic, which means they do not come from living things.

plate tectonics theory .... theory that states that the movement of plates below the Earth's surface drives the geological processes on the surface

rift .... a fault or opening in the Earth's surface

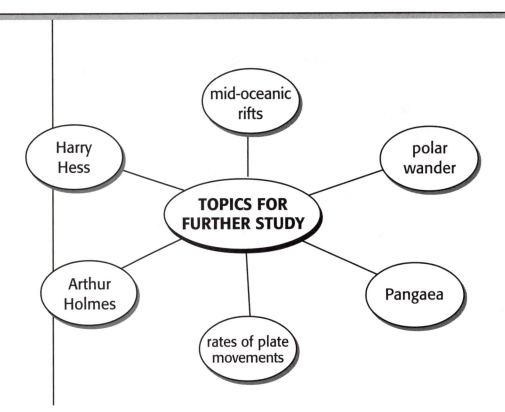

mid-oceanic rifts

Harry Hess

polar wander

TOPICS FOR FURTHER STUDY

Arthur Holmes

Pangaea

rates of plate movements

CHAPTER 3
Earth's Composition

Year	Notable Event
c. 230 B.C.	Eratosthenes measured the Earth using geometry.
A.D. 130	Zhang Heng built a seismograph.
1787	James Hutton identified some rock as having been changed by heat.
1794	William Smith created a geological map of Great Britain.
1797	James Hall demonstrated that igneous rock forms when molten rock cools and crystallizes.
1837	Louis Agassiz coined the term *ice age* to describe past periods of glaciation.
1883	The island of Krakatau exploded in a giant volcanic eruption.
1909	Andrija Mohorovicic discovered the boundary between the Earth's crust and the mantle.
1928	Arthur Holmes hypothesized that heat within the Earth could be driving continental drift.
1968	Scientists began drilling deep under the sea from the vessel *Glomar Challenger*.

Materials per Team

- salt or sugar
- sand
- string
- pencils or sticks
- magnifying lenses
- paper clips
- clear glasses or containers
- warm water

Making Crystals (Igneous Rock)

Learning about Igneous Rock

When liquids cool and become solid, they crystallize. Growing crystals with children will model the process that produces igneous rock, one of three major types of rock. Igneous rocks form as molten rock cools to a solid state. The root word *ignite* reminds us that these rocks are born from fiery lava.

Have students examine powders like salt, sugar, and sand. Use magnifying lenses and microscopes to see the crystalline forms of individual particles. Instruct them to sketch the forms they observe. It may be quite a surprise to some students that the crystals are so beautiful.

Next, let them slowly pour salt or sugar into warm water while stirring. Continue adding the crystals until grains begin to collect on the bottom of the glass and no more will dissolve. As a comparison, have them stir sand in another clear container and be sure they note that it does not dissolve.

Next, students tie one end of a string onto a pencil or a stick, and attach a paper clip to the other end. Suspend the pencil across the top of the glass and let the paper clip sink to the bottom. Observe over the course of a few days as the crystals grow on the string, the pencil, and the sides of the cup. What happens to the paper clip? To avoid rust, use a plastic-coated paper clip or other non-metallic object as a weight.

Crystals can be grown without string using a shallow dish. Have each team make a solution of saturated water (the hotter the water, the more easily the salt or sugar dissolves), pour it into a shallow dish, and let the water evaporate. Salt can be separated and obtained from salt water by this method.

Extend and vary the experiment by using different powders. Compare several kinds of sugar and salt, including epsom salt. As students add sand to water and try to make it dissolve, ask them to imagine how hot the conditions must be to dissolve rock. The sand will lead to the next activity, which is about sedimentary rock.

Mt. Kilauea lava flow crossing road (photograph by R.L. Christianson, U.S. Geological Survey)

R E A D I N G:
Rocks That Cool

What is the Earth made of? To answer, you might begin by making a list and putting things into categories. **Geologists** do that task as part of their jobs. But it is far from easy.

On Earth, **matter** usually exists in one of three forms: **solid, liquid,** and **gas.** Heat, pressure, and chemical activity can all change the forms matter takes over time. To categorize the rocks that make up the Earth, we use clues that reveal their history and formation and help us to group them.

Reading the clues takes lots of practice. Back when geology was a new science, theories about the formation of the Earth varied widely. Two theories about rock formation were popular in the eighteenth century.

Abraham Werner (1750–1817) of Germany believed all rock had formed after a great flood. Particles settled out and became hard rock layers. Werner was known as a **Neptunist,** named after Neptune, the Roman god of the sea, because he thought that oceans once covered the whole Earth. Most parts of his theory were later rejected by geologists. But Werner did popularize the notion of rock in layers and the power of water to dissolve and move minerals.

By contrast, James Hutton (1726–1797) was a **Plutonist,** named after Pluto, the god of the Underworld. Hutton became convinced that much rock formed within the Earth and then came to the surface and hardened. He thought the process was still continuing. He saw places in his native Scotland where **magma** had pushed up into other rock layers.

James Hall (1761–1832), another Scotsman, experimented with Hutton's ideas. Hall melted rocks in his laboratory furnace and proved that many of Earth's structures could be produced by great heat.

Rocks that form when molten rock cools and crystallizes are named **igneous** rocks. The root word *ignite* reminds us that these rocks begin in a fiery form. Scientists have classified rocks into three categories, including igneous rocks.

Back to our opening question, "What is the Earth made of?" Rocks usually consist of a variety of materials, especially **minerals.**

Minerals are naturally occurring nonliving substances. Most minerals form crystals when they become solid.

Crystals are structures formed naturally with molecules connected in regular patterns. Snowflakes are an example of crystals that form in the air. Crystals break into pieces with flat surfaces and precise angles. In rocks, crystals usually grow larger when they cool slowly.

Once you start listing the materials of the Earth, the list will grow quickly. When minerals are refined, or separated, from neighboring materials, they are used for an astounding range of tasks. **Metals** come from the Earth, along with **salts,** fuels, building materials, **clay, sand,** the ingredients for glass. . . . You can imagine how long the complete list would be.

Look around and notice the materials around you. Many of them came from the Earth. If you learn more about these materials and how they get from inside the Earth to their present form, you will hear an interesting story about human engineering.

Vocabulary Words

clay .... small, fine-grained mineral fragments

crystal .... arrangement of matter in which the molecules are lined up in a regular, repeating structure

gas .... state of matter in which molecules have no definite shape and fill whatever space is available

geologist .... scientist who studies the history and structure of the Earth

igneous .... category of rock formed when magma (molten rock) solidifies

liquid .... state of matter having definite volume but taking the shape of the container in which it is placed

magma .... molten rock below the Earth's surface

matter .... anything that occupies space

metal .... a set of elements that are shiny, conduct heat and electricity, and have relatively high melting points

Vocabulary Words *(continued)*

mineral ....naturally occurring solid substance with a specific chemical composition and crystal structure. Minerals are inorganic, which means they do not come from living things.

Neptunist ....one who believed that great flooding shaped the surface of the Earth

Plutonist ....one who believed that heat formed rocks and shaped the Earth.

salt ....a crystallized solid; also a common name for sodium chloride

sand ....loose, granular particles of disintegrated rock

solid ....state of matter having definite shape and volume

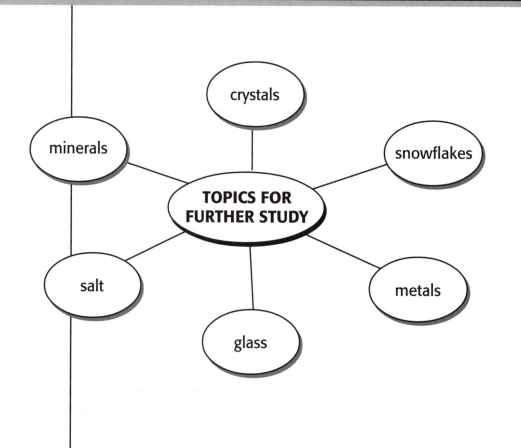

Sedimentary Rock

Learning about Sedimentary Rock

Materials per Team

- variety of samples of sand, pebbles, dirt, dust, shells, and small rocks (reuse the earth materials from the igneous rock activity)

- small transparent vials or cups

- large clear plastic jars or containers (deli containers or clear tennis ball cans work well)

- water

- magnifying lenses

Sedimentary rock, one of three major types of rock, is formed by part of the rock cycle. Mountains and other high lands are eroded by wind and precipitation. Water carries sediments down-hill, where they settle out and form layers. Over the course of many years, the lower layers are compressed and the pressure cements the particles into rocks. Animal and plant remains can become covered by sediment before they decompose, and their forms will be preserved as fossils. (See "Preserved in Stone" on page 64.) In this activity, students will explore sedimentary rock.

Have students carefully examine the samples of materials and add them to the small vials. Then tell them to mix with water and observe the settling process. Have them note the differences between soil and sand. Then have them mix all materials except for one in the jar or container with lots of water. Tell them to place the

cover on the container, invert, and shake. Then they should allow the sandy, rocky material to settle by leaving the container undisturbed. Have them notice the way the particles of matter settle to the bottom and sort themselves into layers.

Ask them to add the material they saved by dropping it into the jar. It forms a layer on top. If they mix up the whole jar again, the layers may change. Remind students that in reality, lower layers may have millions of years to harden. Animal or plant remains trapped in a layer could be preserved and fossilized as the strata (another term for layers) turn to rock. A photograph of the Grand Canyon illustrates the rock strata dramatically.

The layers of rock in this activity tell a story following the theory of superposition. The theory states that layers of rock that are undisturbed by Earth movements lie in the order in which they were deposited. The youngest, or most recent layer, will be on top and the oldest at the bottom. Have students draw the layers that have settled and tell their own story of the rock layers. The shells can represent layers of ancient seabed containing strata formed from the remains of marine organisms.

Grand Canyon rock strata (photograph by C.A. Edwards, U.S. Geological Survey)

READING:
Settling Down

When rocks were found to contain **fossils,** people gained a key to an important discovery. Fossils are the remains of organisms that lived long ago. The rock surrounding the fossil formed about the same time that the organism was alive. So learning about the fossil teaches about the rock, and vice versa. The Earth possesses an enormously long and **dynamic** history. Fossils and their host rock tell a part of that history.

Most fossils are found in **sedimentary** rocks, one of the three major categories geologists use to classify rocks. Sedimentary rocks were deposited in layers. Water and weather break rocks into small pieces and move them. The particles of **mud, clay, sand, gravel,** and sometimes animal remains are squeezed and compacted. They became solid because of **compression** or cementing. The process of rock formation can take millions of years. The root word *sediment* (or think of *sedentary*) reminds us that these rocks were laid down.

The largest, heaviest pieces of rock sink through the water fastest. Water moves smaller, lighter particles more easily and these particles often travel farther. Looking carefully at sedimentary rock can tell scientists how the layers were deposited.

Ancient Greek scientists observed how water moves and deposits particles as long ago as 500 B.C. Nicolaus Steno (1638–1686) made a hypothesis in 1669 that marked the beginning of modern geological study of rock sediments. He called his theory the theory of **superposition.** Steno explained that layers of rock are deposited in order. The oldest layer lies at the bottom and the most recent is found on top.

William Smith (1769–1839) built upon Steno's theory. While doing engineering work throughout England, Smith found similar fossils in different areas of the country. He explained that the rock layers holding similar fossils had formed during the same time period.

Think about how long it must take sedimentary layers to become rock. Some layers that are hundreds of meters thick consist of tiny grains deposited over time. The location of different types of sedimentary rock gives important clues to the natural history of that area. Geologists might theorize that a beach had been in a certain place now covered by sedimentary rock, or that perhaps a mountain range had been ground down over time. The next time you touch and look at sedimentary rock, imagine the Earth's processes that created it and how old that piece of rock might be.

Vocabulary Words

clay .... small fine-grained mineral fragments

compression .... the act of being squeezed and pressed

dynamic .... active and changing

fossil .... the remains of ancient organisms

gravel .... coarse, large-grained sediment

mud .... wet sediments consisting of very small particles

sand .... loose, granular particles of disintegrated rock

sedimentary .... type of rock formed from sediment

superposition .... theory that states that layers closer to the surface are younger than those beneath them, except in the case of extreme folding or other disturbance

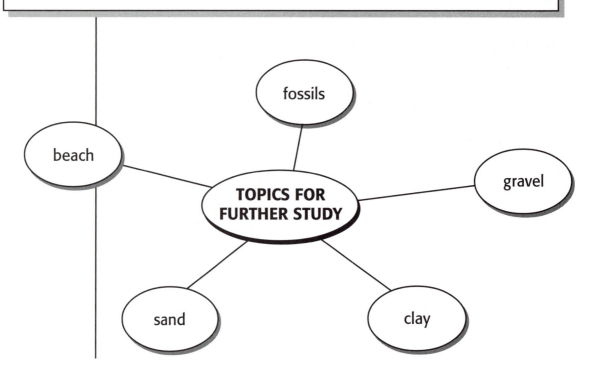

Metamorphic Rock

Learning about Metamorphic Rock

Materials per Team

- small cardboard box or cardboard section
- scissors
- different colors of modeling clay or dough
- samples of gravel, sand, and dirt

Metamorphic rocks represent one of the three major classification categories of rocks. Metamorphic rocks have been changed by pressure and/or temperature. This activity models how forces in the Earth can cause those changes, altering the form of rock.

Students will create a miniature model of the Earth's crust by layering the clay or dough in a small box to represent three or four rock layers. Modeling clay will be rigid enough to be reusable if the students are careful and separate the layers after the activity. Modeling dough demonstrates the viscosity and malleability of the Earth more graphically but probably lasts for one simulation only.

To begin, students will cut off the ends of the box and use them to push in on the layered section of "Earth" to cause folding and uplifting. You can also have students place the model on a large piece of cardboard and then squeeze it by two smaller pieces of cardboard to apply the force. Explain that this demonstration resembles some of the processes that cause geological features to change over long periods of time.

Have the students diagram the layers of clay before and after the rock was metamorphosed. This model works only by pressure and does not produce heat necessary to alter the materials. In reality, metamorphic activity is driven by pressure, heat, or both forces together.

You can use the models to demonstrate three types of tectonic, or large plate, movements. Plate tectonics, a major geological theory of the twentieth century, also creates conditions of high temperature and pressure. Plates are the thin uppermost sections of the Earth's crust that move about slowly atop lower layers. Remake the model, using only two colors and thicker layers to represent plates.

Convergent plates move toward each other. Again, press the ends of the box or two pieces of cardboard inward. This time, have students help one plate override the other, a process called *subduction*. The lower plate goes back into the Earth and is melted. In a different scenario, watch the plates collide and both be pushed upward. This process models how some mountain ranges are formed.

Transform plates attempt to slide past one another. Angle the cardboard pieces while pushing in so the plates pass by each other at a border. This creates friction that causes earthquakes at real fault lines.

To model divergent plates, gently bend the box or cardboard base and use the smaller pieces to push in opposite directions away from the center. A rift is left as the plates move away from each other. Molten material from deeper in the Earth will emerge through a rift and the layers will continue to spread out from the center. Ocean floor spreading is an example of divergent plates at work.

Help students connect their hands-on modeling to the real world using a map showing the plates of the Earth. Find out where the three types of plates can be seen in action in modern times and where scientists think activity occurred in the past. Plate tectonics theory is a powerful investigating tool and has come to be accepted by most scientists.

READING:
Putting the Squeeze On

People often say something is "as hard as a rock." Strong forces in the Earth can change even the strongest rocks. These changed rocks represent one of the three major rock categories and are called **metamorphic** rocks. The root *meta-* means "later" and *morph* means "change."

Metamorphic rocks have been changed by **pressure** and/or heat from their previous structure into a different kind of rock. Geologists investigate how the "parent," or preexisting, rock has become altered by examining its shape, **crystal** structure, and chemistry. Then they can form **hypotheses** about the history of the Earth in that region.

Changes to metamorphic rocks can happen in several ways. Hot **igneous** rock sometimes flows as **magma** and comes in contact with solid rock, affecting its minerals. Other hot fluids from the Earth can create metamorphic rock, too. In other cases, high temperatures and pressures beneath the surface of the Earth cause changes to rock underground. **Stress** occurring at a **fault,** or break, in the Earth can produce heat and force that can then change, or metamorphose, rock.

The surface of the Earth is constantly changing but many of the changes are too slow for us to notice. In 1620, Sir Francis Bacon (1561–1626) of England noted that the coastlines on each side of the Atlantic Ocean seemed to match like pieces of a puzzle. As European exploration of North America increased, mapping became more accurate, and the puzzle pieces looked more likely to fit. But the idea of huge parts of the Earth moving did not make sense.

In the 1890s, Eduard Suess (1831–1914) of Austria proposed that the southern continents were once together in a super continent named Gondwanaland. Suess found that similar fossils could be found on the southern continents, leading him to believe they were all once connected. By 1912, Alfred Wegener (1880–1930) of Germany thought all the continents had been together as one landmass, Pangaea ("all lands"). The concept of a drastically changing Earth surface over time seemed more likely. Discovering the engine for this movement was yet to come.

Most geologists today believe that the outermost layer of the Earth is composed of sections called **plates.** The plates travel around slowly, floating on a layer beneath. In 1929, Englishman Arthur Holmes (1890–1965) explained that heat within the Earth could provide the energy to move the plates. The theory of plate movement is called **plate tectonics.**

The processes of plate tectonics are a major cause of many types of metamorphic rock. Plate tectonics theory changed geology in the twentieth century by explaining how the Earth surface can be in constant movement.

The Earth's plates collide in three basic ways. **Convergent** plates hit head on. Either mountains are pushed up where they meet or one plate slips under the other and down into the hot Earth to be melted. **Transform** plates rub together as they try to slide past one another, causing earthquakes and other movement. **Divergent** plates move apart, often under the sea where new rock flows up from the Earth's interior.

Divergent plates create new ocean floor in a process named **seafloor spreading.** Seafloor spreading can push continents apart. Scientists estimate the rate of movement of different parts of the Earth to be between 2 and 12 centimeters per year. Do the math—how far does a **continent** move in a million years?

Many useful and beautiful rocks are classified as metamorphic rocks, including **marble** and **slate.** Now we have an idea how these rocks form. What other theories will be proposed to explain how the Earth's rocks and surface features are formed and change?

Twisted layers of metamorphic rock
(photograph by Loopack, courtesy of stock.xchng)

Vocabulary Words

continent .... a large landmass on Earth

convergent .... plate boundary in which the plates collide

crystal .... arrangement of matter in which the molecules are aligned in a regular, repeating structure

divergent .... plate boundary in which plates move apart

fault .... a fracture in the Earth's crust

hypothesis .... explanation or theory (plural, *hypotheses*)

igneous .... category of rock formed when magma (molten rock) solidifies

magma .... molten rock below the Earth's surface

marble .... rock created when limestone undergoes metamorphosis from heat and pressure

metamorphic .... rock that has been changed by temperature, pressure, or chemical process

plate .... large segments of the Earth's lithosphere that move around, affecting the surface configuration of the continents, oceans, and other features

plate tectonics theory .... theory that states that the movement of plates below the Earth's surface drives the geological processes on the surface

pressure .... a measure of the concentration of force on a specific area

seafloor spreading .... process in which new seafloor is created under the ocean at a divergent plate boundary. Magma emerges from beneath the seafloor as the plates separate.

slate .... a type of metamorphic rock

stress .... force per unit area on an object

transform .... plate boundary where one plate slides past another horizontally

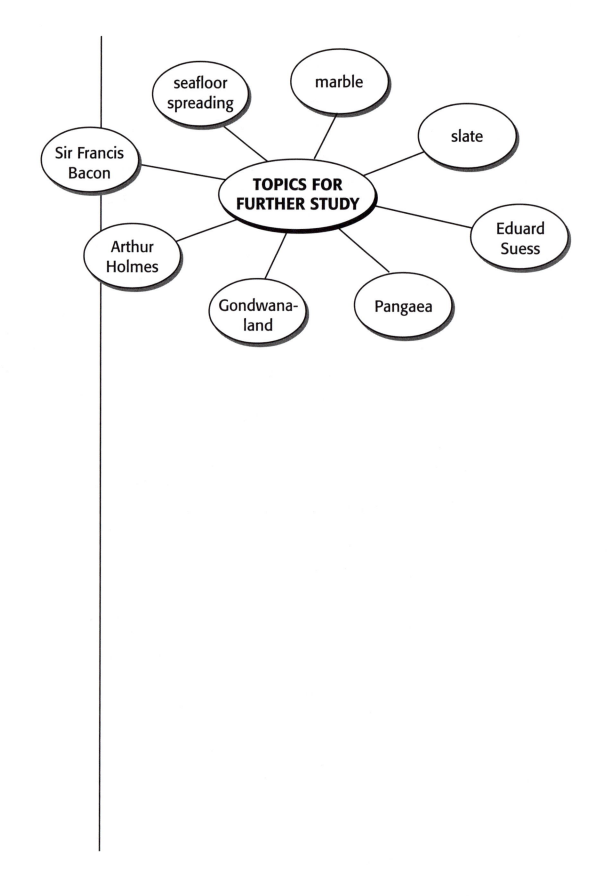

seafloor spreading

marble

slate

Sir Francis Bacon

TOPICS FOR FURTHER STUDY

Eduard Suess

Arthur Holmes

Gondwana-land

Pangaea

Model Earth

Cooking Up a Model Earth

Scientists often need to use clues to solve problems. We can't see into the Earth very deeply, but at some places we do get a glimpse. Ask students where we can see beneath the surface (caves, tunnels, highway cuts, canyons, etc.). Drilling or digging into the Earth provides a cross-section sample and a hint about the types of rock in the crust. This activity will give students an idea of what that is like.

Have the class cook up its own section of the Earth to explore. Mix up several different cake batters and bake cupcakes or loaves with layers of each variety. Add small candy bits in layers also. Do the cooking as a separate activity, especially with some parent volunteer help, and you can have groups of students prepare samples for each other. The object is to have simulated sections of the Earth's crust that students can drill to discover what is beneath the surface.

Materials per Team

- cake mixes (and necessary ingredients)
- small edible bits to add to mixes
- baking tins or cupcake wrappers
- wide-mouthed straws or cardboard tubes from rolls of paper

The baking process represents igneous and metamorphic activity. The model Earth begins in a fluid form (batter), which is heated and then cooled. Layering different batters models sedimentary activity. Advanced modelers might bake their Earth at an angle to simulate faulting. Ask students to suggest other ways to make their models represent geological processes. For example, candy sprinkled on top might stand for a glacial erratic, a boulder carried by giant ice sheets and left behind when melting occurred.

Using the straws, have students drill into the finished cakes to bring up samples. Tell them that these samples simulate the "core" samples brought up by geological drilling teams. Have them try to determine what the composition of the cake is by examining the core samples. Then cut open the cakes to test their accuracy, and eat the results.

READING:
Looking below the Surface

How do we know so much about the composition of the Earth when we live only on its surface? Take a look at a cut-away drawing of the Earth in a geology book or encyclopedia. You will be impressed with the details of the diagram, especially when you realize no one has ever seen the inside of the Earth. As the twentieth century ended, the deepest drill hole into continental crust had gone down only about 12 kilometers.

How deep is 12 kilometers? Not far compared to the radius of the Earth, which is more than 6,000 kilometers. Use a map to discover a place 12 kilometers from your school and imagine digging a hole that deep. Because it is so rare to have a look into the Earth, most of the evidence about our planet's interior comes to us indirectly rather than by observation.

The layers under the Earth's surface are sometimes revealed in places where natural or man-made forces have cut away a path. The Grand Canyon in Arizona is the most famous natural chasm, and people have dug holes for mining and wells for thousands of years. In modern times, engineers have made road cuts and tunnels where rock has been dug or blasted away for a highway or railroad. In 1968 scientists began drilling deep under the sea into the ocean floor. The ship *Glomar Challenger* could work in water as deep as 4,000 meters.

Scientists must often make deductions based on clues. Using small glimpses or pieces of evidence, Earth scientists develop theories about areas that they cannot observe directly. They use tools to explore regions they cannot reach. For example, they plot the behavior of **earthquake waves** traveling through the interior of the Earth to determine the composition of the planet's core. Sending sound waves into the Earth and tracking their return adds to this **sonic mapping.**

Studying the magnetic field around Earth gives another set of clues to what is inside. In 1939, German scientist Walter Elsasser (1904–1991) theorized that currents and flows in Earth's liquid core produce our planet's **magnetic field.**

What have scientists learned about the layers of the Earth through these means? In 1909, Croatian geologist Andrija

Mohorovicic (1857–1936) discovered the boundary between the crust and the mantle, the next layer below. He was studying an earthquake by analyzing the pattern of waves it produced. He found a difference in the **wave velocity** at about 32 kilometers below the surface, marking a place where the composition of rock changes. In his honor, this boundary is known as the **Moho.**

As **seismic** equipment has become more sensitive, scientists make measurements in many parts of the world. The time it takes waves to travel through the Earth gives scientists clues about what kind of rocks the waves passed through. Theories are then developed about the structure inside the Earth.

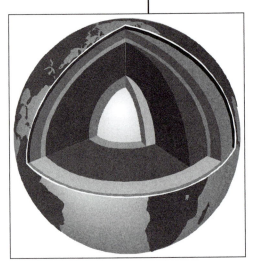

Diagram of Earth's layers

Scientists continue to learn more about the three layers of the Earth: **crust, mantle,** and **core.** You can compare the Earth to an egg which has similar layers: shell, white, and yolk. The upper part of the mantle can be divided into further layers called the **lithosphere** and the **asthenosphere.** The core is believed to have two basic parts, an inner core and an outer core. Look at a diagram of the Earth and imagine how hard it is to visualize layers so deeply hidden.

Abraham Werner (1750–1817) was the most influential **Neptunist** and James Hutton (1726–1797) an important **Vulcanist.** Did giant floods carry rocks to settle out all over the Earth, as Werner thought? Did the heat from the Earth's hot interior cause many landforms, as Hutton described? Discoveries about Earth's layers made Hutton's theories more acceptable. Hot, **igneous** rock from the Earth's interior pushes up and into other layers, where it can be seen. If all rock had settled out of the sea, the igneous rock would not be so **intrusive.**

Louis Agassiz (1807–1873) built a hut and lived on a **glacier.** He helped establish that some rocks are carried great distances by sheets of ice. That explains some of the surface rocks scattered about the countryside. How did layers of rock get to be in mountains high above the surrounding land?

People found shells of sea creatures on mountains. That seemed very confusing and reinforced Neptunist beliefs about all rock being deposited by giant floods. Scientists developed other theories to explain that parts of the Earth are rising or sinking, being built up and broken down. The top of a mountain with fossil sea shells was once beneath the ocean long ago. It would take enormous amounts of time for these processes to occur.

Charles Lyell (1797–1875) helped convince people that the Earth is very old by examining the changes on the surface and calculating how long the processes required. Lyell influenced Charles Darwin's (1809–1882) theory of **evolution.** Darwin was convinced by Lyell's work that nature had enough time to create a diverse set of living things through **natural selection.**

When the Earth formed, it may have been a **molten** mass that gradually cooled and solidified. If so, material that was more **dense** would have settled closer to the core. A French geologist, Gabriel Auguste Daubree (1814–1896), used his knowledge of **meteorites** to suggest that the core of the Earth was composed of an iron and nickel mixture.

From all these clues, scientists have been able to produce a picture of the inside of the Earth. The model fits all data we have so far. Remember that what we think is true today may be disproved in the future. **Plate tectonics theory** was unknown before the twentieth century and has become one of the fundamental ideas of geology. When you make your own model Earth, keep in mind that your facts are based upon what we know now.

Vocabulary Words

asthenosphere .... the layer of the Earth below the lithosphere, believed to be at least partially molten

core .... central part of the Earth

crust .... a layer of the Earth, the outermost layer of the lithosphere

dense .... having high density; thick

earthquake .... violent shaking of the ground caused by waves from underground movement

evolution .... the theory that genetic changes from generation to generation over time cause species to change gradually

glacier .... large mass of ice that lasts for a long period of time

igneous .... category of rock formed when magma solidifies

intrusive .... describing igneous rock that has forced its way into other rock

lithosphere .... the outer shell of the Earth, including the crust and the plates

magnetic field .... the space around a magnet where its force is in effect

mantle .... the section of the Earth between the crust and the core

meteorite .... object from space that has reached Earth

Moho .... short for "Mohorovicic Discontinuity." The Moho is the boundary between the Earth's crust and the mantle.

molten .... melted; made into liquid form by heat

natural selection .... survival of individuals whose characteristics are advantageous for their environment and elimination of individuals who do not succeed

Neptunist .... one who believed that great flooding shaped the surface of the Earth

plate tectonics theory .... theory that states that the movement of plates below the Earth's surface drives the geological processes on the surface

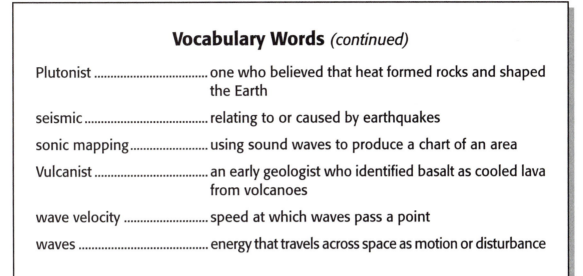

Vocabulary Words *(continued)*

Plutonist .... one who believed that heat formed rocks and shaped the Earth

seismic .... relating to or caused by earthquakes

sonic mapping .... using sound waves to produce a chart of an area

Vulcanist .... an early geologist who identified basalt as cooled lava from volcanoes

wave velocity .... speed at which waves pass a point

waves .... energy that travels across space as motion or disturbance

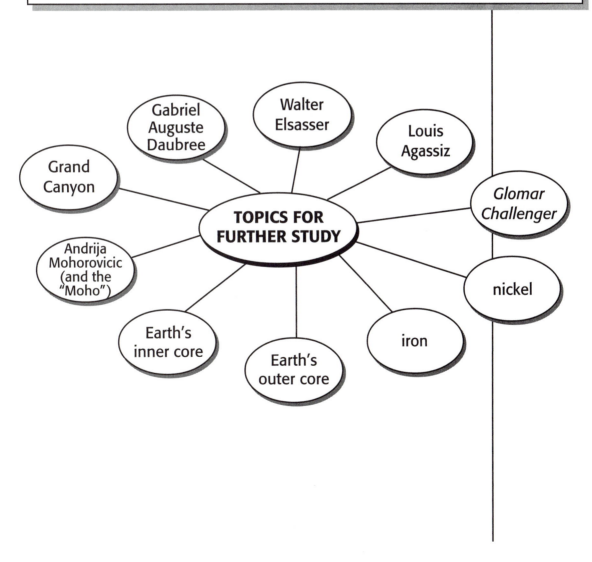

Grand Canyon

Gabriel Auguste Daubree

Walter Elsasser

Louis Agassiz

Glomar Challenger

TOPICS FOR FURTHER STUDY

Andrija Mohorovicic (and the "Moho")

nickel

Earth's inner core

Earth's outer core

iron

Materials per Team

- empty paperboard milk cartons
- samples of sand, gravel, dirt, and small rocks
- water
- freezer
- board or ramp

Glaciers

Ice That Flows

Sometimes rocks are found in places where scientists wouldn't expect them. Glaciers have moved these rocks called *erratics*. Students can simulate the process by building artificial "glaciers" to carry rock to new locations.

Glaciers carry enormous loads of materials scraped from the Earth. As the giant ice masses creep south and north across the Earth responding to climatic changes, they pick up and deposit sediment along the way. Build simulated glaciers by freezing sedimentary material mixed with water in an empty paperboard milk carton. Vary the way students build the glaciers and see how they differ. Have students mix the sediments and rocks with water, pour the mixtures into the containers (leave space for water expanding when it freezes), and put them in the freezer on their sides. Test to be certain the containers will not leak and place them on cookie sheets to be safe.

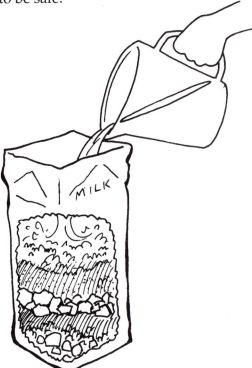

With other containers, have students freeze the water and other materials in several steps to produce some layering. Make one glacial layer, freeze, and then build another on top, freeze again, and so on.

On a warm day outside or over a large container inside, remove the "glacier" from its carton and place it on a slightly inclined board to melt. Students may need to tear the container to separate it from the ice mixture. As the ice melts and slowly slides along the board, the glacier dumps large piles and leaves trails of sediment along its path. You can place sand or dirt on the board to simulate the land beneath the glacier.

Ask students to test their models in different ways and observe the results. Vary the temperature (inside the classroom versus outdoors) and the angle of the slope. Ask students to think about where on the Earth glaciers can be found and how they are alike and different from the models.

Drawing of the southern Alps showing areas of rapidly melting ice

R E A D I N G:
Giant Sheets of Ice

Parts of the Earth are covered by thick sheets of ice called **glaciers.** Glaciers can change the surface of the Earth dramatically. They gouge and tear away layers, carrying rocks along for miles.

As glaciers scour the surface, they sculpt valleys, lakes, hills, and other features. When they melt or retreat, glaciers leave their mark on the land. Rocks moved and left behind by glaciers are called **erratics.** Mountain glaciers are called **alpine,** or **valley, glaciers** while larger ice sheets are called **continental glaciers.**

Swiss-born Louis Agassiz (1807–1873) studied glaciers before much was known about them. By 1837, he had coined the phrase **"ice age."** He discovered that large sections of the Earth were once covered by glaciers that have now melted or shrunk. Agassiz believed strongly in **field study** and found evidence on the modern Earth that helped him form theories about the distant past.

Scientists wonder whether more "ice ages" loom in the future. They study ice from existing glaciers to find clues about ancient climates and to identify predictable patterns. As the twenty-first century began, scientists attempted to understand human involvement in **climate change.** As the average temperature on Earth climbed, questions arose. How much of the change is caused by **carbon dioxide,** or **CO_2,** released by combustion (burning) of **fossil fuels**? How much is a result of other cycles we may not yet understand?

Some theories tie ice ages to **sunspot** cycles. Perhaps the heat energy produced by our sun varies over time. Chinese astronomers recorded sighting sunspots in 165 B.C. An eleven-year cycle was discovered by a German astronomer, Heinrich Schwabe (1789–1875), who began observing sunspots in 1826. In 1848, American Joseph Henry (1797–1878) theorized that sunspots are cooler than the surrounding regions. You should never look directly at the sun, but you can use Henry's method. Poke a pin through one sheet of paper and hold it over another sheet on a sunny day. See if you can project an image of the sun onto the bottom sheet of paper.

Many large mammals that lived on Earth before or during the ice ages are extinct. Imagine a time not too long ago (by an Earth history scale) when **mammoths, sabre-toothed cats, giant sloths,** and other prehistoric animals roamed the land. Some scientists believe the last species of mammoth lived when the Egyptian pyramids were being built in another part of the world. How much did the retreat of glaciers affect their extinction, and how much was the result of human hunters?

Scientists have drawn maps showing where sheets of ice covered North America thousands of years ago. Glaciers still cover parts of the land. When you look at a map and compare the area covered by the remaining glaciers to the area covered during the last ice age, you will see why **global warming** is a concern to modern humans.

Vocabulary Words

alpine glacier	smaller glacier that often flows through mountain valleys; sometimes called *valley glacier*
carbon dioxide (CO_2)	common gas composed of molecules with one carbon atom and two oxygen atoms
climate change	term used to indicate a gradual long-term shift in climate
continental glacier	a large continuous glacier with an area greater than 50,000 square kilometers
erratic	rock carried by a glacier to a spot far from its original site
field study	scientific investigation performed in a natural environment instead of a laboratory
fossil fuel	term for carbon-based fuel deposited in the Earth over time from the remains of organisms
giant sloth	a mammal species that is now extinct
glacier	large mass of ice that lasts for a long period of time
global warming	rise in the average temperature measured at the Earth's surface
ice age	cold period in Earth's history when the planet was covered with numerous glaciers
mammoth	extinct elephant species
sabre-toothed cat	an extinct member of the cat family
sunspot	dark spot on the sun's surface

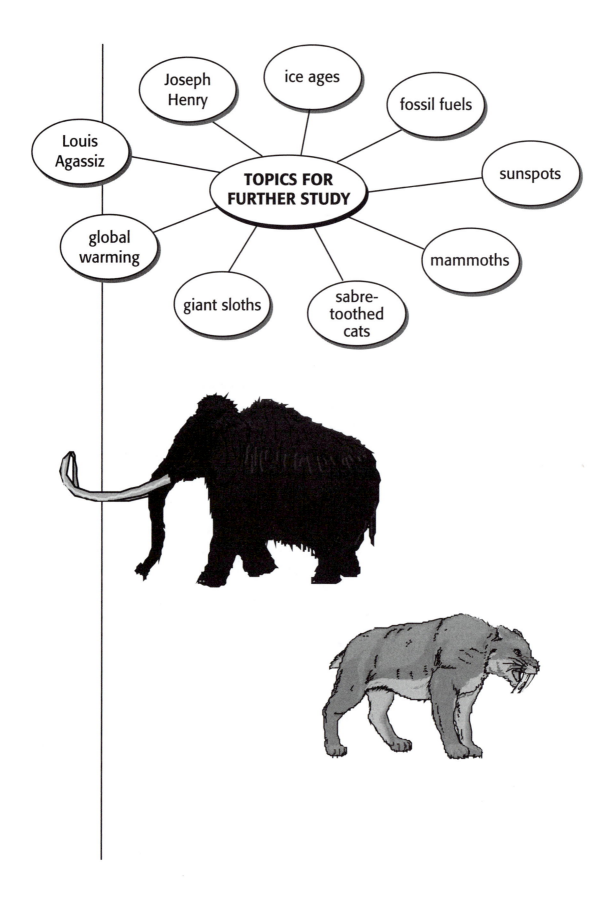

Density

Making a Water Sandwich

Density is the measure of a ratio—how much mass occupies a given volume. How packed together is the matter in a space? This activity demonstrates that lower-density materials float on more dense ones.

Before students arrive for the lesson, fill three empty juice or soda containers with equal amounts of warm water. Add and stir a measured amount of salt into one container (about 200 milliliters if you are using a 2-liter bottle), or use a spoon and begin with six or seven spoonfuls. Add twice that amount of salt to the second bottle, and stir to dissolve. Leave the third container as plain tap water. Color each solution with a different food color.

Divide the solutions so that every group of students will have a container of each liquid. Groups will also need mixing cups for each student to use for testing, and a waste cup per team to collect liquids after testing.

Challenge students to discover the order of density among the liquids. It is best to start testing one color versus one other color, rather than all three at once. They will need to discover which liquid floats on top of the others and which sinks to the bottom.

To demonstrate how liquids layer by density, pour some of the plain-colored water into a clear container holding a small amount of cooking oil. The oil will float on the water, even if you shake or stir it. Caution the students that layering the colored solutions will not be as easy.

Using the droppers or straws, they should pick up a small amount of liquid and add it carefully to their container. To avoid mixing the liquids, warn students not to splash. The best technique is to tip the container and dribble the second liquid down the side (see the diagram on page 106). You may need to demonstrate how to roll a few drops of one liquid from a medicine dropper or straw.

When students are ready, they can add a few drops of one color to another. They should observe carefully whether the colored solution they drop in sinks below or floats upon the water already

Materials per Team

- water
- salt
- food color
- empty juice bottles
- small transparent containers, vials, or glasses
- medicine droppers or plastic drinking straws
- cooking oil for demonstration

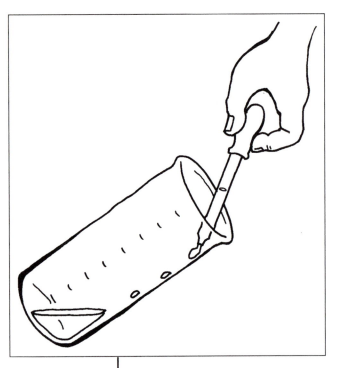

in the container. Be sure they record the outcome. Encourage teamwork so students compare results.

The younger or less careful the students are, the greater the difference in water density needs to be. The liquids may form layers in subtle ways, so dexterity and careful observation are required. Adjust the proportions by increasing the difference in salt amounts for an easier activity. Also, write down the colors and salt proportions so you remember! To challenge older or more capable students, make three colored salt water solutions to compare.

After comparing each liquid individually against the other two in density tests, students can carefully make their liquid sandwiches. The solution with the most salt should form the bottom layer and the fresh water should float on the top. The middle layer of the "water sandwich" should be the colored solution with half the salt of the most dense solution on the bottom. The salt water solutions mix easily, so caution students to work carefully and not become frustrated.

See if each team of students can successfully produce a layered liquid column. Be sure they understand that salt water (salt + water) is more dense than fresh water (water only), because more matter occupies the same space.

R E A D I N G:
What Is Density?

An old trick question asks, "Which weighs more, a pound of feathers or a pound of lead?" Of course, both weigh the same, but what makes people hesitate before answering? It is because of their difference in **density.**

Density is equal to mass divided by volume, or how much "stuff" is packed into a certain amount of space. Feathers are much less dense than lead—a pound of feathers takes up a lot more space than a pound of lead.

Understanding density helps geologists learn more about the composition of the Earth. Scientists study how waves travel through the interior of the planet during and after an **earthquake.** They also use explosions and sound generators to produce more waves to study.

Inside the Earth, layers and segments vary in density. Scientists measure the **wave velocity** from place to place through different parts of the Earth. When the density of the material in the Earth changes, the behavior of the waves changes. The waves bend when they cross the boundary from one layer to another. With enough data and laboratory experiments, geologists can estimate the density and composition of the interior of the Earth.

When **magma** flows beneath the Earth's surface, less dense mixtures can float upon more dense ones. The density of **lava** can affect the behavior of a **volcanic eruption.**

Scientists believe the **continents** float on a layer beneath them called the **mantle.** The **crust** at the ocean floor is more dense. Clarence Dutton (1841–1912) called the process this demonstrates the principle of **isostasy.** The crust rises or sinks depending on the mass and density of the land supported by the underlying mantle.

You will use density to measure many things as you study not only science but other subjects as well. To find the population density of a country or region, you would divide its population by its land area. This is a measure of the average number of people living in each acre, square mile, or other unit of land. When you study geography, divide a region's population by its area and you will have a picture of how close together people live.

The population of major cities is often much larger than the population of entire states in the United States, despite the huge difference in area. No wonder apartment buildings grow so high in big cities—the population density is very high as well.

Vocabulary Words

continent .... a large landmass on Earth

crust .... a layer of the Earth, the outermost layer of the lithosphere

density .... a measure of how much matter is in a given space, or how "tightly packed" that matter is; represented by the formula density = mass/volume

earthquake .... violent shaking of the ground caused by waves from underground movement

eruption .... emerging or being forced out

isostacy .... process by which sections of Earth's crust rise or sink, seeming to float on the mantle below

lava .... molten rock that reaches the surface of the Earth

magma .... molten rock below the Earth's surface

mantle .... the section of the Earth between the crust and the core

volcanic .... from volcanoes, or from rock formed by volcanoes

wave velocity .... speed at which waves pass a point

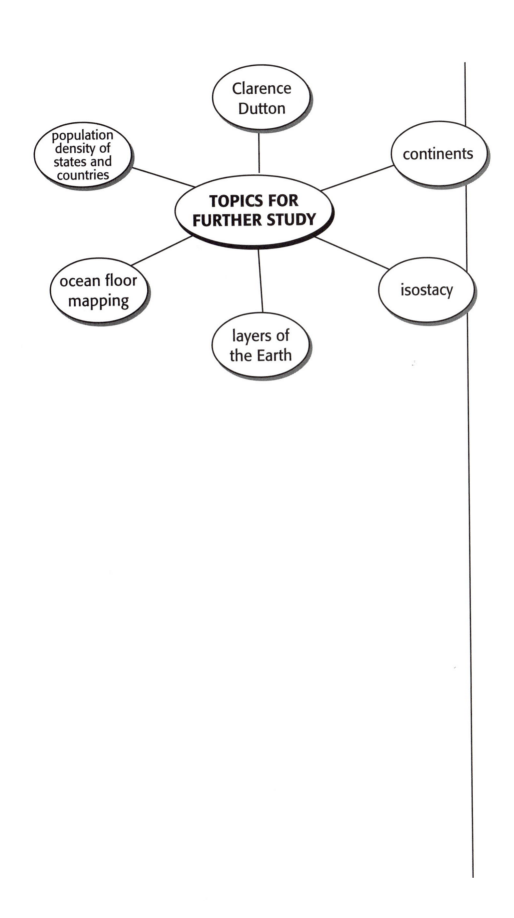

Materials per Team

- Jello®
- small paper bowls
- sand
- modeling clay
- water
- toothpicks and glue
- sturdy table or board

Earthquakes

Earthquake Waves

Waves travel through parts of the Earth at different rates depending upon the composition of the land or underground layer. Some forms of rock transmit waves faster than others. In this activity, students can simulate earthquakes and test the stability of their model buildings.

Prepare Jello ahead according to instructions. Have teams of students construct model houses and other buildings with toothpicks and glue. Try some "skyscrapers" as well as smaller structures. Students can build a base with glued toothpicks and construct the rest of the structure without glue. When earthquakes shake the base, students will observe how much of the building topples.

Fill some bowls with sand, some with Jello, some with modeling clay, and some with water. Stand the student buildings up in the bowls by sticking toothpicks into the materials. Do not place any buildings in the bowl with water. Then you can create earthquakes.

Place the bowls on a board or table. Shaking the board sends vibrations into the bowls and students can see how each medium withstands an "earthquake." Dropping a book or other heavy object onto the board can also cause a tremor and may make a more constant force. Try shaking the bowls by hand—this will especially make the sand shift. What happened to the buildings in each bowl?

The sand represents sediments, often the base for smaller buildings. The Jello simulates the behavior of certain soils and rock that are fairly plastic in composition, especially when subjected to the force of earthquakes. The clay would be stable bedrock, able to move and vibrate during earthquakes but not as likely to shift unless a fault (break) went through it. The water bowls can demonstrate how waves might be created by earthquake activity.

Damaged caused by the 1989 Loma-Prieta, California earthquake (photograph by J.K. Nakata, U.S. Geological Survey)

READING:

How Earthquakes Shake Us Up

Earthquakes are among the most destructive natural acts people have to face. The terror of having the Earth move beneath your feet would be frightening enough, but that is often followed by massive damage. Buildings and other structures fall, utility lines rupture, great quantities of rocks and soil can be dislodged, fires may ignite, and even **tsunamis** can be spawned. But earthquakes have provided scientists with important lessons about the inside of the Earth.

When an earthquake occurs, great sections of the **crust** called **plates** are grinding together. The edge of a plate may be passing over or under another plate or sliding past a boundary of a neighboring plate. Vibrations radiate outward from the collision site. In 1760, John Michell (1724–1793) of England hypothesized that earthquakes were the result of waves from these great rock movements beneath the Earth's surface.

These waves can be detected at great distances by using sensitive devices. Scientists have been building these devices since ancient times. As early as about 130, Chinese scientist Zhang Heng (78–139) had built a machine that indicated the direction of an earthquake. Luigi Palmieri (1807–1896) of Italy built the first modern seismograph, an instrument used to measure earthquake waves, in 1855. In 1880, another Englishman, John Milne (1850–1913), invented a more accurate seismograph, and around the world scientists began to set up networks of detectors.

Earthquake waves provide scientists with much information. Two types of waves travel through the Earth, with each kind telling its own story. Both types of waves can be sensed at remote stations. P waves, or primary waves, arrive first. They behave somewhat as sound waves do in air. They compress, or squeeze, the material they travel through.

S waves, or secondary waves, arrive next. They behave as a wave does when you shake a rope—the movement of the material is at **right angles** to the direction of the wave. For example, tie a ribbon to a rope and stretch the rope out between two people. When one person shakes the rope, waves travel along the rope but the ribbon moves up and down at a right angle to the waves.

A third type of wave arrives and can be recorded at the sensing station. These are called *surface waves.* Surface waves follow the curve of the Earth and travel along the ground. These waves are the last to reach a seismic recording station because they have the furthest to travel and are also the slowest kind.

The **velocities** of the other wave types are different also. P waves are fastest of all and can travel through any material—solid, liquid, or gas. S waves are slower than P waves and do not travel through gas or through the main part of liquids.

Because the waves behave differently, scientists have discovered where the interior layers of the Earth change. One of the first scientists to use P and S waves was Richard D. Oldham (1858–1936), who also suggested that the Earth has a core. In 1909, Andrija Mohorovicic (1857–1936) found the boundary between the crust and the mantle. Beno Gutenberg (1889–1960) found the boundary between the mantle and the outer core in 1914. Inge Lehmann (1888–1993) discovered another discontinuity, or boundary where the wave behavior changed, in 1936. This area marks the change from outer core to inner core. At these great depths, the metallic core of the Earth seems to be solid.

Houses destroyed by the 1989 Loma-Prieta, California earthquake (photograph by C.E. Meyer, U.S. Geological Survey)

In 1935, Charles Richter (1900–1985) developed a scale for the strength of earthquakes. When you hear about an earthquake in the news, listen for the measurement on the **Richter scale** to find out how strong it was.

As the twentieth century went on, scientists learned to create and measure their own waves to test theories about the composition of the Earth. Mapping the ocean floor, hunting for oil, and monitoring weapons testing are just three examples of **sonic** technologies. The prediction of earthquakes remains an unsolved challenge. As new technologies become available, scientists hope to predict accurately when, where, and how strong earthquakes will be.

Vocabulary Words

crust .... a layer of the Earth, the outermost layer of the lithosphere

plate .... large segments of the Earth's lithosphere that move around, affecting the surface configuration of the continents, oceans, and other features

Richter scale .... standard for measuring the size of earthquakes

right angle .... 90˚ angle; square corner

sonic .... related to sound

tsunami .... large wave caused by undersea earthquake

velocity .... the speed and direction of an object over time

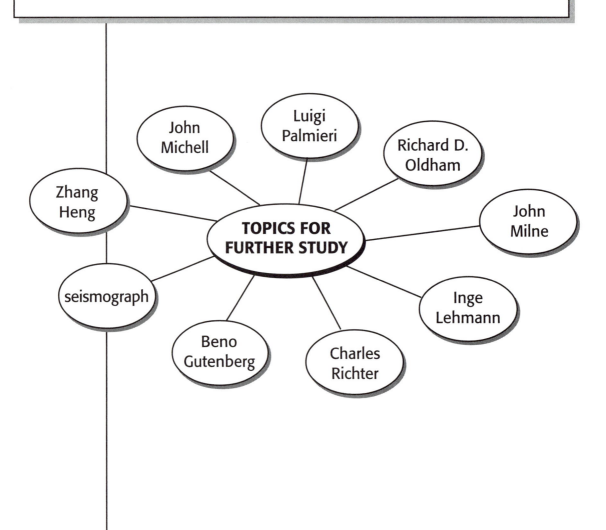

CHAPTER 4
Weather and Climate

TIME LINE

Year	Notable Event
3500 B.C.	Egyptians predicted the start of flood season by the position of stars.
300s B.C.	Aristotle observed that the sun evaporates water.
1592	Galileo Galilei invented a thermometer.
1640s	Blaise Pascal experimented with air pressure.
1643	Evangelista Torricelli invented a barometer.
1686	Edmond Halley made a map of prevailing winds.
1714	Gabriel Fahrenheit established a temperature scale.
1742	Anders Celsius set his temperature scale.
1783	Balloon flight began, allowing people opportunity to travel into the atmosphere.
1783	Horace de Saussure measured relative humidity with a hair hygrometer.
1802	Luke Howard suggested names for clouds based on Latin words.
1935	Radar was invented and became an important tool for weather forecasting.
1960	The United States launched TIROS I, the first weather satellite.

Thermometers

Measuring Heat

Materials per Team

- clear drinking straws
- glass bottles
- markers
- modeling clay
- water
- food coloring

Making this very crude thermometer with water will demonstrate how alcohol and mercury thermometers work. Discussing the problems and inaccuracies of this model will help students understand how improvements have made modern thermometers more accurate.

Have each group fill a glass bottle a little more than half full with water. They can then add food coloring so the water will be easier to see in the straw. Next, they should put the straw into the bottle, leaving part of the straw sticking out, and seal it into the opening with modeling clay. Warn them not to allow the straw to touch the bottom of the bottle. The clay will prevent air from entering the bottle around the straw.

Students should carefully blow into the straw and water will rise into it. Air is being forced out of the straw, allowing water to enter. Have students continue until the water is about halfway up the part of the straw sticking out of the bottle. After a few minutes, mark the water level in the straw with a colored marker.

Set all of the bottles in a warm place, perhaps near a heater or on a sunny windowsill. You could also place them in bowls of very warm water. The air in the bottles heats and expands, forcing more of the water in the bottle to go up the straw. The water in the straw should climb above the mark made at room temperature.

Ask students to predict what happens to the bottle in the refrigerator or in bowls of ice water. Test and see if the water level in each straw goes down when the temperature goes down.

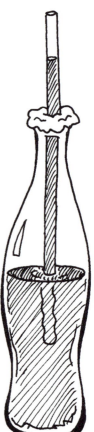

This thermometer might be adequate for roughly comparing temperatures. However, there are a lot of problems doing more than that. Students should be able to brainstorm a list of factors that make this water thermometer an inaccurate scientific instrument.

- Evaporation of water affects water level.
- Air pressure affects water level.
- Because water *expands* when it freezes, freezing could break the device. Ice would not move in the straw anyway.

Discuss what other kinds of thermometers we use and how they work. Assign students to research mercury and alcohol tube-style thermometers, metal springs and strips, and other methods of measuring heat.

R E A D I N G:

Measuring the Temperature

Earth's **climate** may be one of a kind. Our planet provides a unique set of environments for many forms of life. Perhaps one day humans will discover another planet or moon with an **oxygen**-rich **atmosphere** and abundant water. But for now, Earth is the only place we can live without total life support.

Living organisms continue to be found in habitats that were previously believed to be hostile to life. Human explorers use technology to push the limits of discovery farther into remote areas, such as deep undersea chasms and dense tropical forests.

Technological advances have also improved scientists' ability to forecast local weather conditions. Sensitive instruments, some operated by remote control, provide accurate measurements. Communication among weather stations and **satellites** provides large volumes of data for computers to process. All of these sources of information give **meteorologists** the tools to foretell the upcoming weather.

Meteorologists can predict local conditions with some degree of accuracy using visual observation. For example, a pattern of cloud formation might lead to a storm over the course of several hours or a day. But by developing tools for meteorology, scientists can look farther into the future with greater accuracy.

The study of weather using instruments may have begun with the invention of the thermometer, a device to measure heat. Nowadays, we accept that air exists, takes up space, and has a measurable temperature and a measurable pressure. But into the late 1600s, no one had proven that air was a mixture of gases.

Galileo Galilei (1564–1642) knew that gases expanded when heated. He invented a device called a *thermoscope* that measured the changes. But Galileo did not know that the pressure on the air in his thermoscope also changed its **volume.**

In 1714, Gabriel Fahrenheit (1686–1736) used the metal mercury to measure temperature change. Mercury, like air, also expands when heated but is dense enough not to be affected much by air pressure. Fahrenheit's scale is still used today. He set 0° at the lowest point he could reach by freezing salt water.

Using the same kind of thermometer, Anders Celsius (1701–1744) changed the scale. He used a centigrade, or 100° scale. Curiously, Celsius originally set 0° as the boiling temperature of water and 100° as the freezing point, but the scale was quickly reversed. In 1848, Lord Kelvin (William Thomson, 1824–1907) devised a scale with no negative numbers. He set 0° at a temperature he calculated to be the lowest possible. When the lowest possible amount of heat energy is present, the temperature is said to be **absolute zero.**

Other types of thermometers have since been invented and accuracy continues to improve. **Metal** expansion, **electrical resistance,** and other techniques are now common. People were always able to feel changes in temperature but learning how to measure and record them proved to be a long and difficult process.

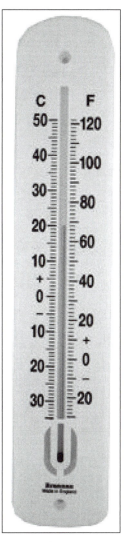

Centigrade and Fahrenheit thermometer

Vocabulary Words

absolute zero .... temperature at which particles have no heat energy, calculated to be about −273° C

atmosphere .... envelope of gases surrounding a body in space

climate .... average weather conditions over a long period of time

electrical resistance .... force that resists the flow of electricity

metal .... the set of elements that are shiny, conduct heat and electricity, and have relatively high melting points

meteorologist .... scientist who studies the atmosphere, including weather and climate

oxygen .... gas that makes up about 21% of Earth's atmosphere

satellite .... man-made or natural object orbiting another object

volume .... a quantity of space occupied by an object or matter

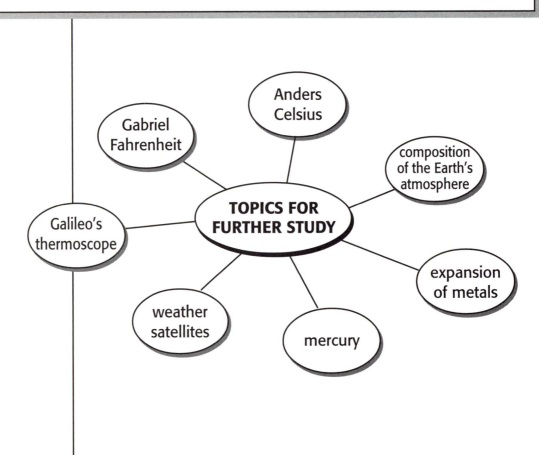

Relative Humidity

How Much Water Is in the Air?

Spill a small amount of water onto a hard surface (spreading some with a sponge onto the chalkboard works well) or pour it into a shallow container. Notice how rapidly it evaporates. Discuss the fate of the water with the students—where did it go?

Water commonly exists in three forms—solid (ice), liquid, and gas (vapor). When it transforms from one stage to another, it undergoes a physical change. The water molecules in our example changed to a gaseous state by evaporating. The opposite change from gas to liquid is called *condensation*.

At different times, atmospheric conditions can cause quicker or slower evaporation of water. Meteorologists can use a device called a *hygrometer* to measure evaporation rates and the resulting value is called *relative humidity*. Relative humidity is expressed as a percentage ratio—what is the current evaporation rate compared to the maximum, or saturation, rate for the current temperature? Stated more simply, how much water is in the air?

At 100% relative humidity, an equal amount of water condenses as evaporates. The air is in effect full of water, so when more water evaporates, an equal amount condenses. Think about a night when fog or mist is in the air.

Conversely, as relative humidity values become lower, there is a greater difference between evaporation and condensation. The air has a high capacity to accept evaporated water without having any condense. Think of a very dry day in the desert when water dries up quickly. By recording and comparing the difference between the temperature of a thermometer with a dry bulb and one with a wet bulb, students can measure relative humidity.

To begin, have each team set up two thermometers. They should wrap the bulb of one with a cloth or paper towel dipped in room temperature water. This one is the wet bulb thermometer. The other will simply measure air temperature, so it will be the dry bulb thermometer. Have students record the temperatures for a twenty-minute period or until the wet bulb temperature becomes steady. They should graph both temperatures on the same pad using different colors.

The wet bulb temperature will be lower because the evaporating water creates a cooling mechanism. Technically, the water's change in state requires energy, which it removes from the air in the form of heat energy.

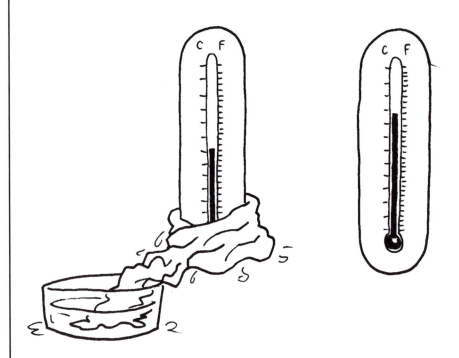

A large difference between temperatures means lots of evaporation is occurring around the wet bulb, lowering its temperature. More water is evaporating than condensing. The relative humidity is low so the air has lots of capacity to accept water vapor.

If the difference between the wet bulb and dry bulb temperatures is small, little evaporation is occurring and relative humidity is high. The air's capacity for water vapor is small. There is no room for newly evaporating water unless some vapor that is already in the air condenses. Use the chart on page 123 to help students convert the temperature data to relative humidity.

Wet and Dry Bulb Table

To determine relative humidity, find the dry bulb temperature on the left and the difference between that and the wet bulb temperature on the top. Where the row and column meet, read the relative humidity as a percentage.

Difference between Dry Bulb and Wet Bulb Temperature

	2	3	4	5	6	7	8	9	10	11	12	13	14	15	16
5	72	58	45	33											
6	73	60	48	35											
7	74	62	50	38	26										
8	75	63	51	40	29	19									
9	76	64	53	42	32	22	12								
10	77	66	55	44	34	24	15	6							
11	78	67	56	46	36	27	18	9							
12	78	68	58	48	39	29	21	12	7						
13	79	69	59	50	41	32	23	15	10						
14	79	70	60	51	42	34	26	18	13						
15	80	71	61	53	44	36	27	20	13	6					
16	81	71	63	54	46	38	30	23	15	8					
17	81	72	64	55	47	40	32	25	18	11					
18	82	73	65	57	49	41	34	27	20	14	7				
19	82	74	65	58	50	43	36	29	22	16	10				
20	83	74	66	59	51	44	37	31	24	18	12	6			
21	83	75	67	60	53	46	39	32	26	20	14	9	6		
22	83	76	68	61	54	47	40	34	28	22	17	11	8		
23	84	76	69	62	55	48	42	36	30	24	19	13	10		
24	84	77	69	62	56	49	43	37	31	26	20	15	12	5	
25	84	77	70	63	57	50	44	39	33	28	22	17	14	8	
26	85	78	71	64	58	51	46	40	34	29	24	19	16	10	5
27	85	78	71	65	58	52	47	41	36	31	26	21	18	12	7
28	85	78	72	65	59	53	48	42	37	32	27	22	19	13	9
29	86	79	72	66	60	54	49	43	38	33	28	24	21	15	11
30	86	79	73	67	61	55	50	46	39	35	30	25	22	17	13

Dry Bulb Temperature

All temperatures are shown in degrees Celsius.

READING:

It's Not the Heat, It's the Humidity

Have you ever heard an uncomfortable person say, "It's not the heat, it's the humidity?" They are suffering not only because the temperature is high but also because the air is damp. Maybe you've heard another weather cliché—"It's hot, but it's a dry heat." That saying downplays the discomfort one feels in high temperatures in dry climates. When the air is dry, heat is not so oppressive. What do these expressions mean, and are they true?

Water is present in air as a **vapor**. We see water **condense** from the air when drops appear on cooling surfaces. For example, a glass holding a cold drink will get wet on the outside. **Dew** forms on low-growing plants and other surfaces when the temperature drops at night and reaches the dew point. These examples also tell us that warm air can hold more water than cool air.

In 1783, Horace de Saussure (1740–1799) used a human hair to tell if the amount of water in the air was high or low. As many people notice when they complain about a "bad hair day," the length of a hair varies according to humidity. Saussure's invention and other devices that measure water vapor content are called *hygrometers.* Some hygrometers compare temperature data from wet and dry thermometers. With that information, you could then read a chart telling **relative humidity** for each difference.

If the air were **saturated,** or full of water vapor, it would be holding as much vapor as possible at that particular temperature. Any new water evaporating makes vapor already in the air condense, or become liquid. Think about a foggy night when the air feels wet. Relative humidity measures the percentage of the maximum water vapor the air is currently holding.

If you can safely get near a heater that is blowing warmed air (a heat vent in a room or the outlet of a clothes dryer will work), try this experiment. Hold your hand in the path of the heated air and notice how warm it feels. Then wet your hand with room temperature or warm water. Place your hand in front of the heater again. How does the air feel now?

Even though the water on your hand is warm and the air hitting your hand is also warm, you feel a cooling from the heater's air flow. That's because the water on your hand is evaporating and that requires energy. Your hand is cooled.

You can measure relative humidity using two thermometers. If you keep the bulb of one thermometer wet and one dry, their temperatures will differ. Some of the water around the bulb of the wet thermometer will evaporate. Measure the two temperatures and plot them on a chart. The greater the difference between the two temperatures, the lower the relative humidity. Can you explain why?

The wet bulb temperature will be lower because the evaporating water creates a cooling mechanism. The water's change in state from liquid to gas requires energy, which it removes from the air in the form of heat energy. As the heat is absorbed by the evaporating water, the temperature around the wet bulb drops.

A large difference between temperatures means lots of evaporation is occurring around the wet bulb. The relative humidity is low so the air has lots of capacity to accept water vapor.

A small difference between the wet bulb and dry bulb temperatures means little evaporation is occurring and relative humidity is high. The air's capacity for water vapor is small. There is no room for newly evaporating water unless some vapor already in the air condenses.

Let's return to our two weather sayings. When someone says, "It's not the heat, it's the humidity," they are probably sweaty and sticky. **Perspiration** is the body's way of cooling itself. Water evaporates from our skin, using heat energy to change from liquid to vapor. The process of cooling is happening in the same way the blowing heater cools a hand in the example described earlier. But on a humid day, the air is closer to saturation, and perspiration evaporates slowly. Cooling does not occur. In a dry climate, water evaporates quickly, so if we perspire, the water evaporates quickly and we feel more comfortable. That means a dry heat is more comfortable than a humid heat. However, some climates are dry but so hot that people still feel uncomfortable. After all, an oven is a dry heat, too!

Vocabulary Words

condense .... to become liquid from vapor

dew .... water that condenses on cooler surfaces

perspiration .... salty liquid released through the skin; "sweat"

relative humidity .... amount of water vapor in the air, described as a percentage of the maximum amount of vapor the air can hold

saturated .... unable to hold any more; completely full

vapor .... gas

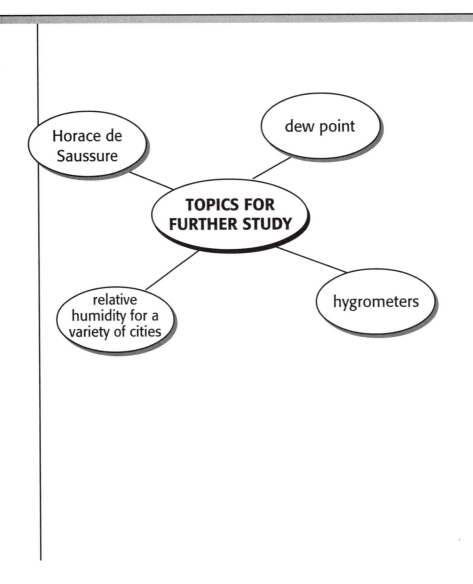

Barometers

Measuring Air Pressure

Air is pressing against us all the time. The force of that pressure varies. A device that measures atmospheric air pressure is called a *barometer*. Students can construct a simple barometer with common materials.

If you have a manufactured barometer to show students, chances are it will have a dial on the front. They can record the changes in pressure from day to day. Record the weather as well, and see if they can find a correlation between the barometer reading and weather conditions.

Their homemade instruments will look different. Here are two ideas for simple barometers.

Materials per Team

- wide-mouthed jars
- balloons
- scissors
- rubber bands
- tape or glue
- drinking straws or oaktag strips
- empty tall milk or juice cartons
- narrow-necked bottles

Method 1

Have students cut a balloon and stretch a piece of it over the mouth of the jar. They can secure it to the jar with a rubber band or two, being sure to keep it pretty tight. Next, they should glue or tape a section of a drinking straw or oaktag strip to the balloon to make a pointer (see diagram on page 128). They can place the jar next to an empty milk or juice carton and mark the spot where the pointer aims on the carton. If you have a class barometer, students can read the current pressure and record it next to the mark on the carton. If you don't have a barometer to check, they can consult a local weather information source for the pressure.

Have students check the instrument each day to see if the pressure changes. Ask what makes the straw or paper arrow point further up or down. (Air pressing down on the balloon makes it change.) Have them record whether it is fair, stormy, or changeable. Keep the barometers in a place where the temperature will remain as constant as possible because heat and cold can cause the balloon to expand and contract.

Once the barometers seem to be responding as either a manufactured instrument or the weather data they've obtained, see if students can calibrate readings onto the carton and make predictions with their balloon barometer. The direction of change rather than the numerical reading often tells more about the future weather. In other words, a rising barometer usually predicts weather becoming fair, while a falling barometer can foretell a storm.

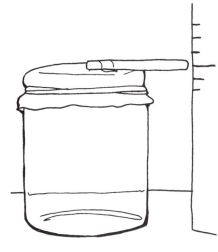

Method 2

Turning over a narrow-necked bottle into a wide-mouthed jar can provide a very simple barometer. Have students make sure the neck of the bottle is in the water but that the mouth does not touch the bottom of the jar. Tell them to look through the jar and see if water has risen into the bottle. After about a half an hour, students should make a mark on the jar with masking tape to record the water level in the neck of the bottle.

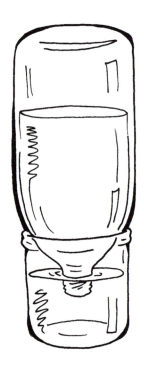

Have them experiment with how much water to use and compare the accuracy to the balloon barometer. Again, temperature can have an effect, and water will evaporate. What can students do to minimize these factors? Setting up this barometer during a time of low pressure is best. That makes it easier to see the change when the weather improves. The water rises as the air pressure rises.

Students may be familiar with ornamental barometers that work in a similar way. Often delicately blown glass sculptures or animal figures with thin necks are designed to be filled with water and hung indoors. By watching the water rise or fall in the narrow part of the sculpture, people can track air pressure.

READING:
At the Bottom of an Ocean of Air

When you dive toward the bottom of a swimming pool, you can feel the water pressing against you. Gravity pulls the water toward the bottom of the pool, and if you are in its way, the water presses on you. If you think about it, we are living near the bottom of an ocean of air. We don't feel it pressing against us because it is always there. But the weight of all those miles of air does exert pressure.

The pressure of the air is not constant. Weather forecasters talk about high pressure and low pressure when they analyze the forecast. Learning to recognize and measure changes in air pressure was one of the most important advances in the study of weather.

Evangelista Torricelli (1608–1648) was a student of Galileo Galilei's (1564–1642). Galileo guided Torricelli in his study of **vacuums.** A vacuum is a place where air has been removed. While investigating vacuums, Torricelli discovered some properties of air pressure.

Torricelli filled a tube with mercury and placed the open end in another container of mercury. The column of mercury in the tube fell to a certain level (about 30 inches) and stopped. Torricelli noted small changes over time. He reasoned that the weight, or pressure, of the air pressing down on the mercury in the container held up the mercury in the tube. When air pressure was high, it pushed mercury farther up the tube than it did when pressure was lower. This basic design of a mercury barometer lasted for centuries.

Very soon afterward, Otto von Guericke (1602–1686) of Germany invented a similar barometer using water. By 1660, he was using his barometer to forecast weather. Von Guericke had a great interest in air pressure and vacuums and became famous for demonstrating the power of the pressure of air. In 1663, he put two copper **hemispheres** together and used his recently invented vacuum pump to remove the air from them. Air pressure on the outside of the resulting sphere pressed the hemispheres together so tightly that two teams of horses could not separate them.

A barometer without liquid is called an *aneroid barometer.* To make this barometer, scientists remove air from a container. They set a pointer in the container to a mark, which will move when there is a change in air pressure.

You can feel air pressure at work by filling a glass with water in a full sink or container. Make sure all the air is out of the glass and turn it open side down in the sink. Gradually lift it toward the surface of the water and watch the water level in the glass. Air pressure on the surface of the water in the container keeps the water in the glass from spilling out.

Think again about the ocean of air. If we move from the bottom toward the top, shouldn't we have less pressure on us? Blaise Pascal (1623–1662) experimented and found that to be true. In 1648, his brother-in-law carried a barometer up a mountain. He recorded that the air pressure reading fell as he ascended.

Barometric pressure is one of the major indicators of weather changes. Stormy weather is usually associated with a falling barometer and low pressure. Fair weather usually accompanies higher readings. Weather systems often swirl in circular patterns. The moving air tends to cause lower pressure toward the center of the swirls and higher pressure toward the outside where the air piles up. Look at a weather map to see where the fronts and storm systems are, and try to locate areas of high pressure.

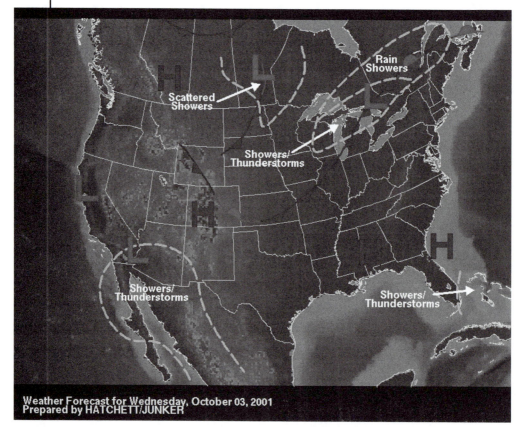

Typical weather forecast map (courtesy of National Weather Service Headquarters and National Oceanic and Atmospheric Administration [NOAA])

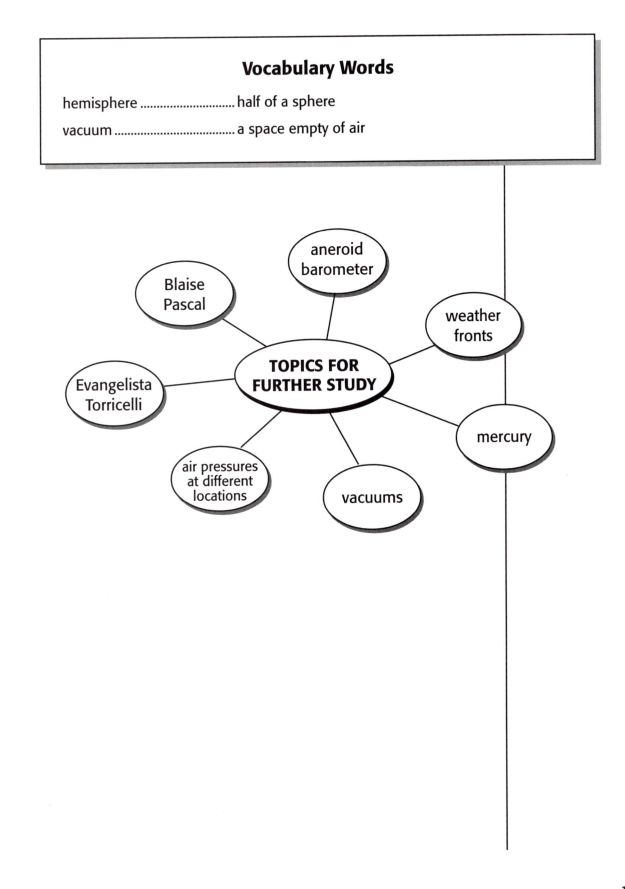

Vocabulary Words

hemisphere .... half of a sphere

vacuum .... a space empty of air

Blaise Pascal

aneroid barometer

weather fronts

Evangelista Torricelli

TOPICS FOR FURTHER STUDY

mercury

air pressures at different locations

vacuums

The Water Cycle

Observing the Water Cycle

From *Science Giants: Earth and Space* © Good Year Books. This page may be reproduced for classroom use only by the actual purchaser of the book. www.goodyearbooks.com

Materials per Team

- four transparent glasses or cups (best if marked with a scale, but not necessary)
- water
- plastic wrap
- graph paper and markers

The water cycle is a primary engine of weather. To study relative humidity and clouds, students will need a basic understanding of the way water is recycled in the atmosphere, a concept that can be difficult to grasp.

Have each group fill four transparent glasses with equal amounts of water. Tell them to cover two of the glasses with plastic wrap and leave two open. If the glasses are not graduated (marked with a scale), have students find a way to track water level. Ideas might include using a ruler to measure every day or marking a scale on the side of glass.

Have them place one covered and one open cup in a sunny location or other warm spot and put the other pair in a cooler, shaded location. They should observe the water levels over the course of several days, using different-colored markers to graph the data over time on their graph pads. Students should notice that the uncovered cups lose water over time. The water level in the open cup in the sun droops faster than the level in the shaded cup.

The water level in the covered cups should be fairly constant. Drops will appear on the underside of the plastic and roll back into the cup. What conclusions can students draw about the behavior of the water?

Because the water in the covered cup evaporates (turns from liquid to gas) and then condenses (turns from gas to liquid), an analogy can be made about the water cycle. On Earth, water is continuously evaporating and condensing. This simple model of the water cycle should help students visualize what is happening outside.

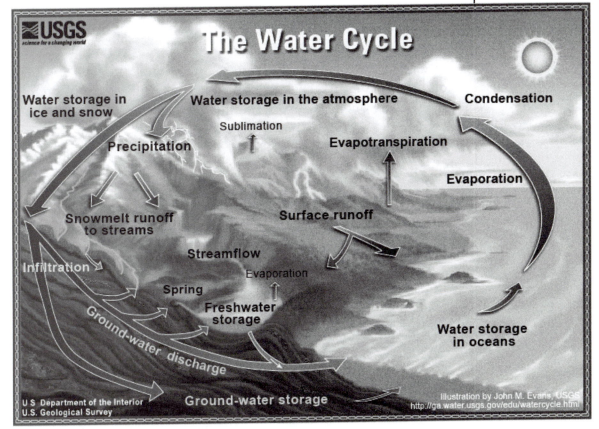

Diagram of the water cycle (illustration by John M. Evans, U.S. Geological Survey)

READING:
Water Gets Around

When you observe a glass of water, you see a colorless, calm-looking liquid. But lots of seemingly invisible activity is occurring. Water **molecules,** made up of **oxygen** and hydrogen **atoms,** are constantly leaving the surface of the water and entering the air. In the air, water molecules form a gas, an invisible form of matter called water **vapor.**

During a hot shower or bath, windows and mirrors in the bathroom frequently "fog up." If you follow the journey of the water, you can trace a mini water cycle. Some water from the shower changes from liquid into vapor. It travels through the warmed air until it comes in contact with the mirror. The vapor **condenses** and turns back to liquid again, as drops or "fog" on the mirror. Later on, it will **evaporate** again as the mirror clears up and becomes dry.

How long have scientists known about water's changeable behavior? It required a lot of creative thinking and experimenting to discover the nature of water. In the late eighteenth century, breakthroughs in chemistry occurred rapidly. Learning that water was a **compound,** or a combination of **elements,** helped solve some mysteries about its behavior.

As often happens in science discovery, one advance led to another. Each new piece of the puzzle added to overall understanding. Here are some highlights of important events:

- Joseph Priestley (1733–1804) burned hydrogen gas in oxygen gas and obtained water. Using an electric spark, Priestley made the hydrogen and oxygen combine.

- Antoine Lavoisier (1743–1794) measured carefully when elements formed compounds, and chemical reactions happened in his laboratory. Total weights stayed the same and **proportions** were fixed, meaning that elements combined in certain specific amounts to form compounds. Water always had the same ratio of hydrogen atoms to oxygen atoms. Lavoisier knew that chemicals could combine or separate but the total amount of **matter** remained constant.

- Henry Cavendish (1731–1810) announced his theory of the composition of water in 1784. Through experimenting, Cavendish reasoned that water was a compound, not an element, and that hydrogen and oxygen proportions were constant at two hydrogen atoms to one oxygen atom. The formula for water (H_2O) looks familiar to us today, but in the eighteenth century, it was a revolutionary discovery.

Because these scientists and others were able to separate out the elements that made up compounds, people began to understand the water cycle more clearly. Air is a combination of gases, and water can change state to be a gas also.

You can do a classroom experiment to prove that water evaporates and you can test whether it happens more quickly at higher temperatures. Because some heat energy is used to evaporate water, our bodies can be cooled by perspiration leaving our skin.

In the **atmosphere,** water leaves the Earth's surface and condenses into clouds up in the cooler heights of the sky. Drops or crystals form and fall back to Earth. The water will evaporate again, cycling through over and over.

Drawing the water cycle is a good way to understand it. What happens to water after it lands on Earth? Remember to include ground water and the release of water vapor by plants and animals.

Iceberg

Vocabulary Words

atmosphere .... envelope of gases surrounding a body in space

atom .... the smallest unit of an element

compound .... in chemistry, a substance made up of the atoms of two or more elements bonded into molecules

condense .... to become liquid from vapor

element .... substance composed of one type of atom

evaporate .... a change from a liquid to a vapor

matter .... anything that occupies space

molecule .... two or more atoms bonded together

oxygen .... gas that makes up about 21% of Earth's atmosphere

proportion .... the amount of a part in relation to the whole

vapor .... gas

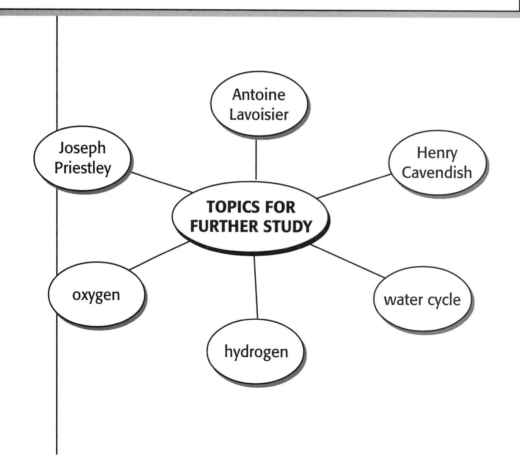

Clouds

Mixing Clouds

Materials per Team

• 1- or 2-liter soda bottles

• stones or gravel

• hot and cold water

• aluminum foil

• ice cubes

• plastic wrap (optional)

Clouds form in response to mixing temperatures and mixing states of matter. Ask the students to recall instances when they've seen clouds form near them on Earth. Examples might include seeing their breath on a cool day, watching vapor condense above a boiling kettle or hot beverage, noticing fog rising or hanging above a lake or river as the sun begins to heat the day, or even seeing the cloud inside the neck of a soda bottle when it's first opened. You can call these clouds "mixing" clouds to differentiate them from sky clouds. When you begin to look for them, you'll find them frequently. Here's a way to produce mixing clouds in the classroom.

Have students cut the top off a plastic soda bottle and fill the bottom with gravel or stones. Next, have them pour in some cold water to keep the bottle from melting. They should then pour in some hot water. Immediately, a cloud will rise from the mixing waters, fogging the sides of the bottle and escaping out the top.

Next, have students cover the opening with aluminum foil, shaping it like a bowl hanging into the bottle. They should place several ice cubes in the foil and observe the system. While waiting for a reaction, students can draw the contraption in their notebooks.

Soon, water drops will form on the underside of the foil. Be sure students understand that the drops do not come from melting ice—the foil is not perforated. Where do the drops come from?

If they've done a water cycle activity (like "Observing the Water Cycle" on page 132), students will surely recognize the familiar process. Water evaporates (turns into a gas) at the bottom of the bottle and condenses (forms a liquid) when it contacts the cold foil. Gravity pulls the drops off the foil and down to the water in the bottom again, where it warms and will evaporate again.

Clouds serve as an intermediate stage, sort of a holding pattern for water. Tiny droplets condensing in the air can come together as clouds. The drops use ice, dust, and other airborne particles to build around until becoming dense enough to fall as precipitation.

READING:
Watching the Clouds Go By

Clouds seem almost unreal as they float through the air. They take the shape of imaginary creatures, and light up with amazing colors at **dawn** and **dusk.** If you haven't noticed the sky lately, check and see what the clouds look like today.

Scientists have been studying clouds for many years. In 1637, Rene Descartes (1597–1650) wrote about how clouds formed. Clouds are composed of **condensed** water **vapor.** Water vapor is a gas. When **relative humidity** is high enough, water vapor will turn into liquid droplets. The droplets group around particles in the air and hold together.

In 1801, Jean Lamarck (1744–1829) classified clouds into five types. But Lamarck's names didn't stick. The names we use to this day were coined in 1803 by Luke Howard (1773–1864). His may not be a household name, but his cloud types certainly are familiar to anyone who has heard a weather forecast.

When Howard was a boy in England, there were two major **volcanic eruptions,** one in Iceland and the other in Japan. For a time, the ash in the sky caused vivid sunsets. Howard also witnessed a spectacular **meteor** streak across the sky, and he was hooked. For much of the rest of his life, he studied the sky and devised the four major cloud names. Howard used Latin names to classify clouds, just as Carolus Linnaeus (1707–1778) did when he classified organisms.

Latin Cloud Name	English Meaning
Cumulus	heap
Stratus	layer
Cirrus	curl
Nimbus	rain

Cloud names may be combined to describe multiple attributes. What do you think **cumulonimbus** clouds are like?

Luke Howard was also one of the first **urban meteorologists.** He wrote a book about the climate of London, noting that conditions in the city were different from those only a few miles away. When modern scientists identify **smog, heat islands,** and other urban weather events, they build on Howard's pioneering work.

Look for clouds in other places besides the sky. Temporary clouds occur where temperatures mix and vapor is present. When you breathe out on a cold day, your breath condenses to form one of these temporary or mixing clouds. Look carefully in the neck of a soda bottle when you open it and you may briefly see a cloud form there. As the sun warms the Earth after a cold night, you might see mixing clouds over a field or pond.

When you watch a cloud, think of Luke Howard seeing clouds as a child and spending his life studying them. If you are really interested in something, follow that interest and see where it will lead.

Low resting clouds in mountain valley (photograph by Captain Albert E. Theberge, NOAA Corps [ret.], National Oceanic and Atmospheric Administration)

Vocabulary Words

condense .... to become liquid from vapor

cumulonimbus .... very dense, tall, menacing clouds, especially dark at lower altitudes

dawn .... the beginning of daylight

dusk .... time when daylight fades

eruption .... emerging or being forced out

heat island .... urban area where air and surface temperatures are higher than surrounding region

meteor .... small object traveling through space

meteorologist .... scientist who studies the atmosphere, including weather and climate

relative humidity .... amount of water vapor in the air, described as a percentage of the maximum amount of vapor the air can hold

smog .... smoke mixed with fog; a form of pollution

urban .... referring to cities

vapor .... gas

volcanic .... from volcanoes, or from rock formed by volcanoes

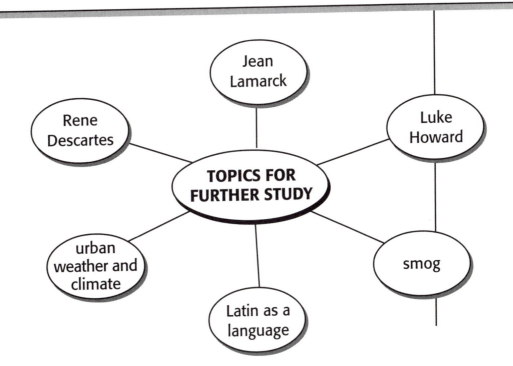

Trade Winds

Learning about Prevailing Winds

From *Science Giants: Earth and Space* © Good Year Books. This page may be reproduced for classroom use only by the actual purchaser of the book. www.goodyearbooks.com

Materials per Team

- warm water
- cold water
- food coloring
- transparent cups
- straws or medicine droppers
- globes
- photocopied world maps

Optional

- turntables (use old record players or "lazy susan" rotating tables)
- marbles or other small spheres
- thermometers

Weather describes atmospheric conditions over a short time span. Climate describes conditions in a generalized, long-term context. Using these activities, guide students to think about why the different parts of the world experience a range of climates.

Temperature Differences

Wind is caused by a variety of factors. Heat from the sun provides much of the energy to move air. Many students will say "hot air rises." Can they demonstrate it? Perhaps you can measure temperature in different parts of the classroom, comparing the amount of heat near the floor to the amount near the ceiling. (Watch your variables—proximity to heat source, direct sun, ventilation currents, etc.). Carefully burn a candle and observe how the wavy lines rising above the flame (Schlerein lines) indicate the movement of air.

Have students set up a simple experiment using four cups of water. Tell them to let two cups come to room temperature and leave them colorless. Then they should fill another cup with warm water and add red food color. Last, they should fill the fourth cup with chilled water and color it blue. If they have thermometers, they can measure the temperatures.

Have students predict what will happen when a few drops of the red water are added to one of the plain water cups. What will happen when blue water is added to the other plain water? Have them use medicine droppers or straws to add the water and record the results. Because water and air are both fluids, tell students that air behaves in a similar way to the water in this activity. When fluids of different temperatures come into contact, movement occurs.

Coriolis Effect

Another engine for wind is the Coriolis effect. Ask students to imagine rolling a ball across a rotating surface. They can test their predictions if you have an old turntable, a lazy susan tray or table, or some other rotating equipment to use. Let them roll marbles across the moving surface and watch as their paths curve.

Some playgrounds have a small merry-go-round for students to ride. Students can roll a tennis ball across the merry-go-round while it spins and observe the path of the ball. If none of the rotating equipment is available, present the problem as a mind experiment and talk it through with students while they sketch their predictions. The deflection, or curving of an object's path caused by the rotation of the Earth, is called the *Coriolis effect*.

Prevailing Winds

Cold air sinks near the poles and heads toward warmer latitudes. The Earth is rotating toward the east. On a globe, have one student gently draw a finger down from the North Pole toward the Arctic Circle, simulating the wind. Meanwhile, a partner should slowly rotate the globe in an easterly direction. Have students note the path of wind. The curving trail of the first student's finger demonstrates the Coriolis effect. Switch roles and try the same activity at the South Pole.

At the equator, where the sun is most direct, air rises and heads toward the poles. This action leaves behind a low pressure area, drawing wind blowing from the tropics toward the equator. Use the globe again to demonstrate how the Coriolis effect tends to create trade winds curving westward as they head toward the equator in the warmest regions. In the Western Hemisphere, the equatorial winds blow from the northeast to southwest. In the Southern Hemisphere, the equatorial winds blow southeast to northwest.

Mid-latitude winds lie between the other two processes. Some of the warmed air from the equatorial region continues north, creating a third cell of trade winds. Trace with a finger through the temperate zones heading toward the poles to show how the Coriolis effect bends winds eastward in the mid-latitudes.

Give students a photocopied world map to draw the general pattern of the trade winds. Many other factors complicate climate modeling, so encourage students to study further and research topics.

Big Dipper (courtesy of NASA, Johnson Space Center, Earth Sciences and Image Analysis)

READING:
Which Way the Wind Blows

How does it feel to be an explorer? Imagine standing at the edge of the ocean. You're pretty sure the Earth is round, so if you sail out far enough, you'll hit land. But you don't want to sail in circles—how will you know where you are and which way you are going?

Every position on the Earth can be described by a clever, imaginary grid system. Picture the Earth in space with one pole "up" and the other "down." Lines of **latitude** travel across and around the Earth in a **lateral** east–west direction like a set of **parallel** belts. The widest belt around the middle of the Earth is named the **equator,** which is line 0°.

Distant stars and the sun both provide travelers with means to compute latitude. Polaris, known as the North Star, always appears in the northern sky over the North Pole. Polaris is easy to find in a dark sky. Draw a line through the two stars on the end of the Big Dipper, and extend the line toward Polaris, which begins the handle of the Little Dipper. Polaris does not change position as the other stars and planets do. If you measure the distance, in degrees, between Polaris and the **horizon,** you will know about how many degrees north of the equator you are.

There are similar navigation techniques using stars for the Southern Hemisphere. During midday, the position of the sun in relation to the horizon can be used to calculate latitude, although the changing of the seasons makes that process more complicated than using Polaris.

Longitude is even more complicated. In the model of a grid system on a globe, lines of longitude run north and south, meeting at each pole. They are all equally long and come together, as opposed to the parallel lines of latitude.

Columbus and other explorers noticed changes of longitude by slight **compass** changes, caused by the Earth's **magnetic field.** But it was necessary to measure time accurately in order to find east–west position more precisely.

Because the sun shines on only part of the rotating Earth at any time, the time of day varies depending on where you are. If explorers could compare the time of day where they were versus the time of day in the place they began their journey, they could know how far they had traveled. Nowadays, we have instruments that tell time accurately, and the Earth is divided into different time zones. But the explorers did not know the exact time and found it difficult to determine how far east or west they were compared to any landmark.

Dutch geographer Reiner Frisius (1508–1555) understood that clock time and local sun time could be compared to compute longitude. But while Frisius wrote about doing that in 1533, actually building accurate timepieces was another matter. About two hundred years later, British clockmaker John Harrison (1693–1776) produced **marine chronometers** that could be used for navigation. Sailors could set Harrison's clocks in the harbor before the voyage, and they would then know the time for their home port for months at a time. When it was noon at sea, they could read the marine chronometer and figure 15° longitude change for each hour's difference (360° longitude around the world divided by 24 hours in a day).

Think about being the explorer setting out upon the ocean again. Even if you know where to go, how will you get there? Wind was the engine, and learning the prevailing winds could make the difference between a successful voyage and extreme hardship. At the same time Harrison and others were enabling sailors to pinpoint their positions, George Hadley (1685–1768) began to explain why the winds on Earth blow as they do.

The **Hadley Cell** models how air circulates in the equatorial region. The sun warms the Earth, causing the air above the surface to rise. It heads toward the cooler poles, leaving a **low pressure zone** behind. As the air cools and falls, it creates high pressure and causes a flow back toward the equator. In 1853, James Henry Coffin (1806–1873) identified three wind zones in the Northern Hemisphere.

These cells of prevailing winds became familiar to explorers and sailors. You can sketch them or study them on a map and appreciate how **transoceanic** routes became more reliable and voyages became quicker. But heat creating pressure differences doesn't tell the whole story.

The Earth's rotation generates another force that creates prevailing winds. The process is called the *Coriolis effect*, described in 1835 by French physicist Gustave-Gaspard Coriolis (1792–1843). Coriolis explained that objects and fluids traveling across a moving body are deflected and follow a curving path.

Dutch meteorologist Christoph Buys Ballot (1817–1890) and American William Ferrel (1817–1891) each independently produced models for wind direction and air pressure. They found that when you place your back to the wind, a **high pressure zone** will be to your right and a low pressure zone to your left. (Reverse this law in the Southern Hemisphere.) Wind speed was rated on a 0–12 scale by Sir Francis Beaufort (1774–1857) in 1805, an important step in standardizing weather measures.

Gradually, as the forces creating prevailing winds became better understood, the study of weather and climate grew increasingly accurate. Areas on the same parallel of latitude can experience very different conditions. Check the coordinates for a city you know. Then find other places on the Earth equally north or south of the equator. How can the climates differ so much despite receiving equal hours of daylight annually? Often, the cause is a prevailing wind.

Many other factors affect climate. For example, as he collected data on his scientific voyages, Alexander von Humboldt (1769–1859) learned about the effect of altitude upon climate. Have you ever climbed a mountain or visited a location at a high altitude? As you travel high above sea level, the climate conditions change, making it seem as if you are farther away from the equator. What other reasons can you think of to explain the variation in climate around the world at various latitudes?

Vocabulary Words

chronometer .... accurate precise clock

compass .... instrument used to determine direction

equator .... imaginary circle around the Earth, halfway between the North and South poles

Hadley Cell .... system of air circulation in which warm air rises near the equator and flows toward the poles, sinking as it cools

high pressure zone .... area of the atmosphere in which air pressure is high, pressing down on the Earth's surface with greater than average force

horizon .... the place where the Earth and sky appear to meet

lateral .... sideways

Vocabulary Words *(continued)*

latitude .... parallel imaginary lines around the Earth providing one of two coordinates for locating points. The equator is latitude 0° and the poles are 90° north and south latitudes.

longitude .... imaginary lines around the Earth that provide one of two coordinates for locating points. Lines of longitude are drawn from pole to pole with 0° longitude crossing Greenwich, England.

low pressure zone .... area of the atmosphere in which air pressure is low, pressing down on the Earth's surface with lower than average force

magnetic field .... the space around a magnet where its force is in effect

marine .... referring to the sea

parallel .... being an equal distance apart at every point on a line or line segment; never intersecting

transoceanic .... across the ocean

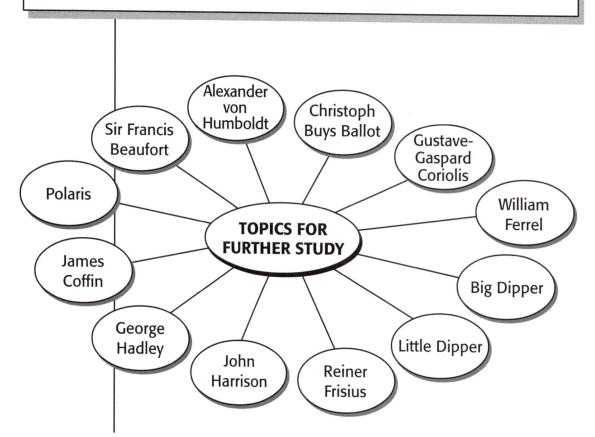

Bibliography

Astronomy Magazine. Waukesha, WI: Kalmbach Publishing.

Ferris, Timothy. *Coming of Age in the Milky Way.* New York: William Morrow, 1988.

Gribben, John. *Almost Everyone's Guide to Science.* New Haven: Yale University Press, 1999.

Gribben, John. *The Scientists.* New York: Random House, 2002.

Hazen, Robert M., and James Trefil. *Science Matters.* New York: Doubleday, 1991.

Hellemans, Alexander, and Bryan Bunch. *The Timetables of Science.* New York: Simon and Schuster, 1988.

Meadows, Jack. *The Great Scientists.* New York: Oxford University Press, 1996.

Panek, Richard. *Seeing and Believing.* New York: Penguin Books, 1998.

Press, Frank, and Raymond Siever. *Understanding Earth.* New York: W. H. Freeman, 1994.

Raymo, Chet. *365 Starry Nights.* Englewood Cliffs, NJ: Prentice-Hall, 1982.

Seeds, Michael A. *Stars and Galaxies*, 2nd ed. Pacific Grove, CA: Brooks/Cole, 2001.

Simmons, John. *The Scientific 100.* Secaucus, NJ: Citadel Press, 1996.

Glossary

absolute zero .... lowest possible temperature. Temperature at which particles have no thermal energy, calculated to be about −273° C.

alpine glacier .... smaller type of glacier than continental glaciers. Alpine glaciers often flow through mountain valleys. Sometimes called *valley glacier*.

antiquity .... ancient times

asteroid belt .... band of small rocky objects orbiting the sun between the orbits of Mars and Jupiter

asthenosphere .... the layer of the Earth below the lithosphere, believed to be at least partially molten

astronomical .... having to do with objects outside the Earth

atmosphere .... envelope of gases surrounding a body in space

atom .... the smallest unit of an element

binoculars .... optical device used for magnifying objects at distances. Binoculars consist of two telescope-like tubes, one for each eye.

calendar .... system of measuring and recording time, especially years

carbon dioxide (CO_2) .... common gas composed of molecules with one carbon atom and two oxygen atoms

catastrophism .... theory that the surface of the Earth was formed by a series of catastrophic events such as floods and volcanic eruptions

cell .... the smallest, microscopic-sized unit of organisms

Cepheid variable star .... giant stars that display a cycle of varying brightness

chemical .... relating to chemistry, having to do with the structure and properties of matter; also a term for a substance used in a chemical reaction or process

chronometer .... accurate precise clock

clay .... small fine-grained mineral fragments

climate .... average weather conditions over a long period of time

climate change .... term used to indicate gradual long-term shift in climate

coal .... the hardened remains of ancient plants, metamorphosed into a hot, burning fuel

coma .... the "head" of a comet

comet .... small, icy body that orbits the sun

compass .... instrument used to determine direction

compound .... in chemistry, a substance made up of the atoms of two or more elements bonded into molecules compression .... the act of being squeezed and pressed

condense .... to become liquid from vapor

continent........................... a large landmass on Earth

continental drift .... the movement of continents relative to each other

continental glacier .... a large continuous glacier with an area greater than 50,000 square kilometers

convergent........................... type of plate boundary in which the plates collide

core...................................... central part of the Earth

cosmology .... branch of science dealing with the creation and evolution of the universe

creation story .... tales and explanations told to explain the formation of the Earth and other natural phenomena

crust .... a layer of the Earth, the outermost layer of the lithosphere

crystal .... arrangement of matter in which the molecules are aligned in a regular, repeating structure

crystallized .... having formed crystals

cumulonimbus .... very dense, tall, menacing clouds, especially dark at lower altitudes

dawn .... the beginning of daylight

decay .... break down into component parts

deluge .... a great rain or flood

dense .... having high density; thick

density .... a measure of how much matter is in a given space, or how "tightly packed" that matter is; represented by the formula density = mass/volume

dew...................................... water that condenses on cooler surfaces

dinosaur .... "monstrous lizard," general name for a variety of extinct reptiles that lived more than 65 million years ago

divergent .... moving apart

dogma.................................. a set of ideas to be believed

dusk .... time when daylight fades

dynamic............................... relating to energy, motion, force, or change

earthquake .... violent shaking of the ground caused by waves from underground movement

electrical resistance .... force that resists the flow of electricity

element .... substance composed of one type of atom

equator .... imaginary circle around the Earth, halfway between the North and South poles

erosion................................ process by which rock and soil are loosened and carried away

erratic .... rock carried by a glacier far from its original site eruption...............................emerging or being forced out

evaporate...........................a change from a liquid to a vapor

evolution theory...............the theory that genetic changes from generation to generation over time cause species to change gradually

extrapolate.........................carry calculations further

fault.......................................a fracture in the Earth's crust

field study...........................scientific investigation performed in a natural environment as opposed to using a laboratory setting

fossil.....................................the remains of ancient organisms

fossil fuel...........................term for carbon-based fuels deposited in the Earth over time from the remains of organisms

gas...state of matter in which molecules have no definite shape and fill whatever space is available

geologist..............................scientist who studies the history and structure of the Earth

giant sloth...........................extinct mammal species

glacier...................................large mass of ice that lasts for a long period of time

global warming.................rise in the average temperature measured at the Earth's surface

gravel....................................coarse, large-grained sediment

gravity..................................force of attraction between objects based on their mass

Hadley Cell.........................system of air circulation in which warm air rises near the equator and flows toward the poles, sinking as it cools

half-life................................time period over which half the amount of a radioactive element will decay

heat island..........................urban area where air and surface temperatures are higher than surrounding region

heliosphere.........................vast magnetic bubble surrounding the solar system, the solar wind, and the magnetic field around the sun

hemisphere..........................half of a sphere

high pressure zone..........area of the atmosphere in which air pressure is high, pressing down on the Earth's surface with greater than average force

horizon................................the place where the Earth and sky appear to meet

hypothesis...........................explanation or theory

ice age.................................cold period in Earth's history when the planet was covered with numerous glaciers

igneous.................................category of rock formed when magma solidifies

impact crater......................geologic features caused by large objects from space crashing into the surface of a planet or moon

intrusive..............................describing igneous rock that has forced its way into other rock

isostacy................................process by which sections of Earth's crust rise or sink, seeming to float on the mantle below

lateral .... sideways

latitude .... parallel imaginary lines around the Earth providing one of two coordinates for locating points. The equator is latitude 0° and the poles are 90° north and south latitudes.

lava .... molten rock that reaches the surface of the Earth

Linnaean classification
system .... system for categorizing organisms. Using this system, scientists identify each species with a two-part name that reflects a general and specific group.

liquid .... state of matter having definite volume but taking the shape of the container in which it is confined

lithosphere .... the outer shell of the Earth, including the crust and the plates

longitude............................... imaginary lines around the Earth that provide one of two coordinates for locating points. Lines of longitude are drawn from pole to pole with 0° longitude crossing Greenwich, England.

low pressure zone............. area of the atmosphere in which air pressure is low, pressing down on the Earth's surface with lower than average force

Magellanic Clouds............. galaxies visible from the Southern Hemisphere

magma .... molten rock below the Earth's surface

magnetic field..................... the space around a magnet where its force is in effect

magnetism .... having the properties of a magnet

mammoth............................... extinct elephant species

mantle................................... the section of the Earth between the crust and the core

marble .... type of rock created when limestone undergoes metamorphosis from heat and pressure

mare..................................... Latin for "sea," a term used to describe and name the flat plains on the moon

marine .... referring to the sea

matter .... anything that occupies space

metal .... the set of elements to the left of a line on the periodic table. Most metals are shiny, conduct heat and electricity, and have relatively high melting points.

metamorphic .... type of rock that has been changed by temperature, pressure, or chemical process

meteor .... small object traveling through space

meteorite .... object from space that has reached Earth

meteorologist .... scientist who studies the atmosphere, including weather and climate

Middle Ages .... historical period in Europe, approximately the years A.D. 500–1500

Milky Way............................ spiral galaxy containing our solar system millennium .... a period of a thousand years

mineral .... naturally occurring inorganic (not from living things) solid substance with a specific chemical composition and crystal structure

mnemonics .... devices, symbols, reminders, and so on, that can be used to help remember something

Moho .... short for "Mohorovicic Discontinuity." The Moho is the boundary between the Earth's crust and the mantle.

molecule .... two or more atoms bonded together

molten .... melted, made into liquid form by heat

mud .... wet sediments consisting of very small particles

natural selection .... the survival of individuals whose characteristics are advantageous for their environment and elimination of those individuals who do not succeed

naturalist .... scientist who studies natural objects and organisms

Neptunist .... one who believed that great flooding shaped the surface of the Earth. Compare to Plutonists, who believed volcanic activity was more instrumental.

Newtonian telescope .... telescope that magnifies an image by reflecting light off mirrors

orbital motion .... the path of an object as it revolves around another object

orbited .... traveled around

oxygen .... gas that makes up about 21% of Earth's atmosphere

parallel .... being an equal distance apart at every point on a line or line segment; never intersecting

perspiration .... salty liquid released through the skin; "sweat"

plate .... large segments of the Earth's lithosphere that move around, affecting the surface configuration of the continents, oceans, and other features

plate tectonics theory ...... theory that states that the movement of plates below the Earth's surface drives the geological processes on the surface

Plutonist .... one who believed that heat formed rocks and shaped the Earth. Compare to Neptunism, which proposed that flooding determined the form of the Earth's surface.

pressure................................ a measure of the concentration of force on a specific area

proportion .... the amount of a part in relation to the whole

pulsar .... a source of radio energy from space, believed to be a rotating neutron star

quasar .... quasi-stellar object; small but powerful source of energy

radioactive .... describes material that emits radiation from the nuclei (plural of nucleus) of its atoms

radiometric dating .... method of determining age of ancient material by measuring the ratio of radioactive elements remaining in the sample compared to elements formed as the radioactive material decays

reflecting .... bouncing off; throwing back

refracting .... bending of light as it passes from one medium to another

relative humidity .... amount of water vapor in the air, described as a percentage of the maximum amount of vapor the air can hold

renaissance .... a revival, a reawakening of cultural achievement

Richter scale .... standard for measuring the size of earthquakes

rift .... a fault or opening in the Earth's surface

right angle .... 90° angle; square corner

sabre-toothed cat .... an extinct member of the cat family

salt .... crystallized solid, common name for sodium chloride. Other salts are compounds formed by combining acids and bases.

sand .... loose, granular particles of disintegrated rock

sanitation .... behaviors designed for public cleanliness and health; prevention of dirty and harmful buildups

satellite .... man-made or natural object orbiting another object

saturated .... unable to hold any more; completely full

seafloor spreading .... process in which new seafloor is created under the ocean at a divergent plate boundary. Magma emerges from beneath the seafloor as the plates separate.

sedimentary .... type of rocks, formed from sediment

seismic .... relating to or caused by earthquakes

shuttle spacecraft .... vehicles designed to enter space and return so they can be flown multiple times

slate .... a type of metamorphic rock

smog .... smoke mixed with fog; a form of pollution

solar wind .... atoms and ions blowing from the sun outward through the solar system

solid .... state of matter having definite shape and volume

solution .... evenly distributed mixture of two or more substances

sonic .... related to sound

sonic mapping .... using sound waves to produce a chart of an area

space junk .... orbiting remnants of man-made objects in space

space station .... a long-term manned satellite designed for scientific research

spectrum .... sequence or range of energy by wavelength

speculation .... the act of contemplating or thinking about something and forming an opinion

speed .... rate at which distance is traveled by an object speed of light .... approximately 300,000 kilometers per second (186,000 miles per second) in a vacuum

speed of waves .... see wave velocity

sphere .... solid round figure

stress .... force per unit area on an object

subduction .... process by which an oceanic plate slides beneath an overriding plate as the two collide

sunspot .... dark spot on the sun's surface

supernova .... explosion of a star

superposition .... theory that states that layers closer to the surface are younger than those beneath them, except in the case of extreme folding or other disturbance

tectonic plates .... large segments of the Earth's lithosphere that move around, affecting the surface configuration of the continents, oceans, and other features

telescope .... an instrument for detecting and viewing distant objects

thermodynamics .... study of the relationship between heat and other forms of energy

transform .... the type of boundary where one plate slides past another horizontally

transoceanic .... across the ocean

tsunami .... large wave caused by undersea earthquake

uniformitarianism .... theory that states that the processes occurring on Earth now are similar to those that affected the Earth in the past

urban .... referring to cities

vacuum .... a space empty of air

valley glacier .... see alpine glacier

vapor .... gas

velocity .... the speed and direction of an object over time

volcanic .... from volcanoes, or from rock formed by volcanoes

volcano .... an opening in the Earth's crust where molten rock and gases erupt

volume .... a quantity of space occupied by an object or matter

Vulcanist .... an early geologist who identified basalt as cooled lava from volcanoes

wave velocity .... speed at which waves pass a point

wavelength .... distance between identical parts (for examples, crests or troughs) of waves

waves .... energy that travels across space as motion or disturbance